P9-DUI-949

ARISTOTLE: PROTREPTICUS

A RECONSTRUCTION

Anton-Hermann Chroust

UNIVERSITY OF NOTRE DAME PRESS • 1964

Copyright © 1964 by the
University of Notre Dame Press
Notre Dame, Indiana

Library of Congress Catalog Card
Number 64-13283
Manufactured in the
United States of America

To

My Friends and Colleagues

of the Yale Law School

FOREWORD

This little book is a straightforward presentation of the likely content of Aristotle's "lost" *Protrepticus*. Written primarily for the use of students of philosophy rather than for the enlightenment of the classical scholar, it makes no pretense whatever to original scholarship or critical evaluation. Nor does it treat the often highly involved and still not completely resolved problems connected with the reconstruction and interpretation of the *Protrepticus*. Such has been done by a number of outstanding scholars, some of whom are mentioned in the list of recommended readings. The author has freely drawn upon Ingemar Düring's *Aristotle's Protrepticus: An Attempt at Reconstruction* (1961), which in his opinion is the most remarkable and up-to-date discussion and presentation of this subject. He has widely utilized Düring's selection and arrangement of the fragments. The translation of these fragments as well as the "Brief Comments," however, are his own. Also, in the interpretation of the fragments, especially as regards their dependence on Plato, the author often disagrees considerably with Düring. Anyone wishing to engage in a more penetrating treatment and study of the *Protrepticus* and the many problems it poses should consult Düring's splendid work, where he will find a most minute critical apparatus, many detailed annotations, and an exhaustive bibliography.

This book is divided into three parts: Part One contains a general Introduction implemented by a list of ancient Testimonia, a list of Collections of the Fragments, a list of the Sources of Reconstruction, and a list of Recommended Readings; Part Two consists of a translation of the Aristotelian texts; and Part Three is made up of Brief Comments to the several texts. The numbers of the comments correspond to the numbers of the fragments.

The author wishes to acknowledge his indebtedness to Professor Francis D. Lazenby of the Classics Department at the University of Notre Dame, and to four of the author's students, Mr. John G. Gaine, Mr. Frank D. McConnell, Mr. Martin K. Gordon, Mr. Michael W. Messmer, and Mr. Charles H. Dunphy, for their invaluable assistance. The book is dedicated to his friends and colleagues of the Yale Law School, where the author spent several delightful months in an atmosphere of relaxed competence, pleasant association, and unrivalled scholarship.

Anton-Hermann Chroust
University of Notre Dame
August 1, 1963

CONTENTS

CONTENTS

INTRODUCTION

Among the so-called early or "exoteric" writings of
Aristotle, the most important is probably the *Protrepticus*. That a *Protrepticus* was composed and "published" by Aristotle has been attested by a number
of ancient authors. Although the original composition
has been lost in its entirety, one is able to reconstruct
it with a fair degree of accuracy—not only in its es-
sential content but also in its main narrative—from a
mass of surviving "fragments," that is, from what can
reasonably be identified as references to, or excerpts
from, this work.

The *Protrepticus* is addressed (dedicated?) to
Themison, a little known "king" or "prince" who about
350 B.C. ruled somewhere on the island of Cyprus.
It is a "hortatory" composition or eulogy which contains a sustained and apparently systematic argument
in favor of a life devoted to philosophy. In view
of certain indisputable similarities and connections
that exist between Aristotle's *Protrepticus* and Isocrates' *Antidosis,* it is fair to assume that these two
writings are approximately contemporaneous. The *Antidosis* was published probably in 353-352 B.C., but
scholars disagree as to whether the *Protrepticus* is a
reply to the *Antidosis,* or whether the *Antidosis* constitutes a refutation of the *Protrepticus.*

It is generally held that Aristotle's earliest works
were dialogues rather than discourses. In the case of

the *Protrepticus,* however, some serious doubts have
been raised as to whether this composition was originally a dialogue. Some scholars insist that it was a
dialogue, and that the ancient "reporters" whose references or citations constitute the preserved fragments
of the *Protrepticus* had suppressed the dialogue form.
They base their view on the fact that the Alexandrian
lists of Aristotle's writings enumerate the *Protrepticus*
among the first nineteen Aristotelian works, all of
which are said to have been dialogues. In addition, it
has also been claimed that Cicero's *Hortensius,*
which is a hortatory debate between two discussants
about the value of philosophy, is a close imitation
of the Aristotelian *Protrepticus.* Those scholars who
maintain that it was a plain discourse point out that
between 360 and 350 B.C. the expository form of
demonstration began to replace the dialogue in scientific demonstrations; however, the dialogue was still
employed effectively whenever the author wished to
survey different or opposing opinions about a particular topic. Thanks to the efforts of the political and
forensic orators as well as the literary influence of Isocrates' writings—especially that of his so-called Cyprian discourses—by about the middle of the fourth
century B.C. the "hortatory essay" (*logos protrepticos*)
had come into vogue.

The surviving fragments indicate that the language,
style, and internal structural arrangement of the *Protrepticus* could very well be Aristotelian. In any event,
the suggestion that they are wholly "un-Aristotelian"
lacks adequate confirmation. It must be borne in
mind that these fragments are often cast in the
diction of the citator and as such at times reveal the
language, style, and even the method of the compiler,
excerptor, or reporter. But it is most unlikely that

the whole surviving text is the product of imitators or forgers. It is, rather, a collection of excerpts and, occasionally, of almost verbatim reports from an authentic Aristotelian composition: the *Protrepticus*. The overwhelming majority of the fragments underlying this reconstruction of the Aristotelian *Protrepticus* has been drawn from Iamblichus' *Protrepticus,* a Neo-Platonist who died about 330 A.D. It is an indisputable fact, ascertainable from his other philosophic writings, that the ideas and notions expressed by Iamblichus in his *Protrepticus* go far beyond the somewhat limited and modest intellectual range of his own philosophic achievements. This fact in itself suggests that in his *Protrepticus* he is using or reporting ideas advanced by other and more talented thinkers—in our case those originally advocated by Aristotle. This does not imply, however, that the several fragments lifted from Iamblichus' *Protrepticus* are literal quotations from Aristotle's original *Protrepticus.* On the contrary, in all likelihood a great many of these fragments are abbreviated, condensed, and, not infrequently, severely mutilated renditions of Aristotle's ideas. To make matters worse, Iamblichus is, as a rule, a fairly poor stylist as well as a muddled thinker, who could hardly do justice to Aristotle's literary and philosophic achievements. Hence, the obvious inadequacies of style and expression as well as the frequent awkwardness in the formulation of philosophic ideas found in the *Protrepticus* of Iamblichus may not be attributed to Aristotle who, in the considered judgment of competent ancient authors and literary critics, expressed himself with great elegance and admirable clarity in his exoteric compositions.

The internal structure of the various arguments advanced by the author of the *Protrepticus* definitely

is akin to that used by Aristotle in his preserved
works, especially—as A. Mansion has pointed out—
to Aristotle's "successive approximation." Starting with
a certain proposition, the argument reaches a pro-
visional conclusion. Then, a new proposition is intro-
duced which likewise is discussed, though perhaps on
a different "level," until it coincides with the provi-
sional conclusion reached in the first argument. Finally, the several arguments are "co-ordinated" for the
purpose of reaching a final conclusion. The subject
matter, the philosophic treatment, and the philosophic
content of the *Protrepticus*, it will be noted, are of a
type one might very well expect from an active
though apparently somewhat independent member
of Plato's Academy around the middle of the fourth
century B.C.

Many a learned and at times heated discussion has
been launched as to whether the *Protrepticus* is
essentially a "Platonic" or an "Aristotelian" composition—whether at the time Aristotle wrote the *Protrepticus* he still adhered to the basic doctrines of
his teacher Plato, or whether he had already begun to
develop his own philosophic system. By adducing
weighty evidence and employing much ingenuity, different scholars have championed widely differing and
even mutually irreconcilable views on this intricate
and most difficult subject. We shall not enter into a
discussion of this extremely involved problem which
may never be fully resolved. It does appear, however,
that a large number of passages found in the *Protrepticus* betray Plato's influence, although in individual instances this has been disputed by some scholars.
But it may be contended that reasonable similarities
exist between Aristotle's *Protrepticus* and Plato's *Euthydemus, Phaedo, Cratylus, Republic, Phaedrus, The-*

aetetus, Philebus, Laws, Epinomis, and the *Greater Alcibiades.* Perhaps *Euthydemus* 278E-282D, which is definitely a hortatory or protreptic discussion, supplied Aristotle with his main theme or, at least, influenced some of the basic notions which he put down in the *Protrepticus.* In the *Euthydemus* Plato maintains that all men strive after happiness; but happiness does not consist of worldly goods, earthly possessions, good fortune, or worldly success; philosophic wisdom alone makes men happy; but this philosophic wisdom is not "useful" in a practical, worldly sense, unless it is applied the right way; only the right kind of philosophic knowledge should guide our actions, and we must always seek that which is good in itself; only rational or philosophic knowledge and true or philosophic wisdom will enable us to distinguish between what is good in itself and what is merely useful as a means to some good; philosophic wisdom can be acquired, and it can make men happy; hence it is necessary for men to pursue philosophy and philosophic wisdom.

Since the Aristotelian *Protrepticus* may very well be called a "mirror of princes," there also exists the possibility that it might in part be under the influence of Antisthenes. Antisthenes composed a number of protreptic works which, as regards their basic tenor, were probably intended as a "mirror of princes": the *Cyrus,* the *Cyrus or On Sovereignty* (Diogenes Laertius VI. 16), the *Cyrus or The Beloved,* and the *Cyrus or The Scouts* (Diogenes Laertius VI. 18), to mention only a few titles. In addition, he wrote *On Justice and Courage: A Hortatory or Protreptic Essay in Three Books* (Diogenes Laertius VI. 16). But, barring a few doubtful fragments and some not altogether reliable secondary sources, all the writings of

Antisthenes are completely lost. Hence it is well-nigh impossible to establish with any degree of certainty whether and to what extent Aristotle's *Protrepticus* might have been influenced by Antisthenes.

No one will seriously contest that some definite connections exist between Aristotle's *Protrepticus* and Isocrates' *Antidosis*. The *Antidosis*, like the *Protrepticus*, is a hortatory essay which, it appears, set a definite literary pattern for future hortatory discourses or dialogues. In addition, the *Protrepticus* seems to be a "reaction" to the *Antidosis*. But the respective aims of these two compositions are substantially different: the *Antidosis* advocates a life of temperance and (practical) justice, while the *Protrepticus* pleads for a life wholly dedicated to philosophy. "In my opinion," Isocrates insists (*Antidosis* 271), "a man is wise who . . . is able to find the best 'middle-of-the-road' course, and I hold that a man is a philosopher if he occupies himself with those studies from which he will most speedily gain that sort of knowledge." Aristotle counters this statement by insisting (*Protrepticus*, frag. 47 Chroust) that "the philosopher alone lives with his gaze on nature and the divine . . . [H]e will try to tie his life to what is eternal and unchanging . . . and will live as the master of his own [soul]."

The *Protrepticus*, it should be noted, in all probability became gradually "lost" when due to the alleged rediscovery or recovery of the esoteric or "doctrinaire" compositions of Aristotle during the latter part of the first century B.C. (Apellicon of Teos, Tyrannion of Amisos, Andronicus of Rhodes, and others), the literary and scholarly interest suddenly shifted to the dogmatic works, subsequently known as the traditional *Corpus Aristotelicum,* at the expense of the

early or exoteric Aristotelian writings. The latter came
to be more and more neglected and ignored, and,
as a result of this neglect, became "lost." But it must
be remembered that for some time the *Protrepticus*
had a considerable influence on the intellectual life
of Late Antiquity and Early Christianity. In fact, it
seems to have enjoyed a considerable popularity
among ancient and Early Christian authors.

According to the testimony of Diogenes Laertius
(V. 22), the *Protrepticus,* which is listed as the twelfth
item in the catalogue of authentic Aristotelian compositions, contained only one "book." By employing a
rather complex method of computation, Paul Moraux
(*Les Listes Anciennes des Ouvrages d'Aristote,* 1951,
pp. 192-193) has established that in its original Greek
version the average "book" (often only a "chapter"
in our terminology) among the works of Aristotle
contained approximately 751-808 (and in some instances more) lines of about thirty-six letters each.
If Moraux's calculations are only approximately correct (there exists no compelling reason why we should
not accept his findings), then we can be fairly confident that we have recovered by far the greater part,
and optimistically speaking, perhaps even the whole,
of the "lost" *Protrepticus* of Aristotle. The several
texts of the "fragments" which are collated here (and
which we believe on the whole to be genuine) total
about 900 lines of approximately thirty-six letters
each. This would make it a reasonable book by the
standard set by the ancient catalogues listing the compositions of Aristotle.

Naturally, any attempt to present adequately the
original text by relying on surviving fragments will
always be defective or, at least, incomplete to some
extent. That certain parts of the original *Protrepticus*

are probably still missing can neither be denied nor
affirmed with any degree of certainty. But unless
new materials should be unearthed, it could be contended that all or nearly all of the really significant
passages have been recovered. Also, the frequently
abrupt transitions from one "fragment" to another,
not to mention the few instances of incomplete sen-
tences or missing words, would indicate that we
are not yet, and perhaps never will be, in the possession of a perfect and complete text. And, finally,
some scholars would undoubtedly suggest the elimina-
tion of a number of "fragments" which are incorporat-
ed in this text, while others, again, might wish to include additional materials.

The sequence in which the several "fragments" are
presented in the main follows the arrangement suggested by I. Düring. It seems to be dictated by the
logical (or rhetorical) development of the argument
itself. But here, too, some scholars might prefer a different and, perhaps, better sequence. The problem of
arranging this sequence has long been hotly debated.
Some scholars believe they have discovered in Iamblichus' "reports" (contained in his *Protrepticus*, edit. H.
Pistelli) three major groups corresponding to chapter
VI (p. 36, line 27 to p. 41, line 5), chapters VII and
VIII (p. 41, line 6 to p. 54, line 9), and chapters
IX, X, XI and part of chapter XII (p. 54, line 10 to
p. 60, line 10 or p. 61, line 4) of Iamblichus' *Protrepticus*. Others, following what appears to be a
"logical coherence" or "rhetorical sequence," would
arrange the fragments or excerpts recovered from
Iamblichus' *Protrepticus* as follows: pp. 36,27-37,22
(Pistelli); pp. 49,1-51,6; pp. 51,16-52,5; p. 51,6-15;
p. 52,6-16; pp. 34,5-35,18; p. 36,7-20; pp. 37,22-40,1;
p. 41,6-15; pp. 52,16-56,12; pp. 40,1-41,5; pp. 41,15-43,

25; pp. 43,27-44,9; p. 43,25-27; pp. 44,26-45,3; p. 44, 9-26; pp. 56,13-60,10; and pp. 45,4-48,21. Others, again, simply accept the sequence observed by Iamblichus.

The *Protrepticus,* as such a title would indicate, is both an eloquent eulogy of speculative philosophy and an exhortation to live the "philosophic life," that is, a life dedicated to speculative philosophy. The most exalted of all human endeavors, we are told, is directly related to the most noble part or aspect of human nature, namely, to reason and to the intellectual part (or activities) of man's soul. It is this reason, this intellectual aspect, that makes man most closely resemble God. It is only through reason that man may ever hope to taste the greatest possible pleasures: intellectual contentment and spiritual joy which come from the possession of philosophic wisdom and philosophic insight. All other faculties, virtues, and joys of man, including all earthly goods, are forever subordinate to this philosophic wisdom, to philosophic insight, and to true philosophic knowledge. In the Islands of the Blessed, so the story goes, man will enjoy the beatific vision in the perfect and undisturbed contemplation of absolute truth. But in this sorry world of ours the most exalted and, at the same time, the most necessary concern of man consists in philosophic wisdom and philosophic knowledge, man's closest approximation to the beatific vision while yet on earth.

TESTIMONIA

The ancient authors who attest to the fact that
Aristotle composed a work entitled *Protrepticus* are
Stobaeus, *Florilegium* IV. 32. 21 (p. 785, edit. O.
Hense), who quotes Teles (*Teletis Reliquiae*, p. 45,
edit. O. Hense); Alexander of Aphrodisias, *Commentaria in Aristotelis Topicorum Libris Octo* (edit. M.
Wallies, 1891), in: *Commentaria in Aristotelem Graeca* (hereinafter cited as *CIAG*), vol. 2, part 2, p. 149,
lines 9-17; Olympiodorus, *Commentarius in Platonis
Alcibiadem Priorem* (edit. F. Creuzer, 1821), p. 144;
Elias (*olim* David), *Commentaria in Porphyrii Isagogen et in Aristotelis Categorias* (edit. A. Busse, 1900),
in: *CIAG*, vol. 18, part 1, p. 3, lines 17-23; David,
Prolegomena et in Porphyrii Isagogen Commentarium
(edit. A. Busse, 1904), in: *CIAG*, vol. 18, part 2, p. 9,
lines 2-12; Diogenes Laertius, *Lives and Opinions of
Eminent Philosophers* V. 22 (title 12); *Vita Hesychii*
(or, *Vita Menangiana* or *Vita Menagii*, Hermippus),
title 14; Ptolemy (El-Garib), *"Catalogue of Aristotle's
Writings"* (Andronicus), 1-2; Anonymous, *Scholia in
Aristotelis Analytica Priora*, Cod. Paris. 2064, fol. 263ᵃ;
and, perhaps, Cicero, *De Finibus Bonorum et Malorum* V. 4. 11.

COLLECTIONS OF THE FRAGMENTS

The extant fragments of the *Protrepticus* have been
collected by V. Rose, *Aristotelis qui ferebantur librorum fragmenta* (1886), quoted as Rose; also in vol. 5
of the Berlin Academy Edition of Aristotle's Works
(1831); R. Walzer, *Aristotelis Dialogorum Fragmenta, in Usum Scholarum* (1934), quoted as Walzer;
W. D. Ross, *Aristotelis Fragmenta Selecta* (1955),

quoted as Ross, translated in W. D. Ross, *The Works of Aristotle,* vol. 12 (1952); and I. Düring, *Aristotle's Protrepticus: An Attempt at Reconstruction* (Studia Graeca et Latina Gothoburgensia, vol. 12, 1961), quoted as Düring.

SOURCES OF RECONSTRUCTION

The ancient authors, "reporters," or sources from whom the fragments of the *Protrepticus* have been retrieved, are: Stobaeus, *Florilegium* III. 3. 25 (p. 200, edit. O. Hense), quoted as Stobaeus III. 200; Stobaeus, *Florilegium* IV. 32. 21 (p. 785, edit. O. Hense, and *Teletis Reliquiae²,* p. 45, edit. O. Hense), quoted as Stobaeus IV. 785; Grenfell-Hunt, *The Oxyrhynchus Papyri* IV. 666, quoted as *Oxyrh. Papyr.* IV. 666; Alexander of Aphrodisias, *Commentaria in Aristotelis Topicorum Libris Octo* (edit. M. Wallies, 1891), in: *CIAG,* vol. 2, part 2, p. 149, lines 9-17, quoted as Alex. Aphrod., *Top.*; Iamblichus, *Protrepticus* (edit. H. Pistelli, 1888), p. 34, line 5 to p. 60, line 10, quoted as Iamblich., *Protrep.*; Iamblichus, *De Communi Mathematica Scientia Liber* (edit. N. Festa, 1891), p. 79, line 15 to p. 83, line 5, quoted as Iamblich., *Math. Scient.*

RECOMMENDED READINGS

I. Bywater, "On a Lost Dialogue of Aristotle," *Journal of Philology,* vol. 2 (1869), 55-69.
H. Diels, "Zu Aristoteles' Protreptikos und Cicero's Hortensius," *Archiv für Geschichte der Philosophie,* vol. 1 (1888), 477-497.
E. Villa, "Il *Protreptikos* di Aristotele," *Rediconti dell'Istituto Lombardo,* Classe di Lettere, Scienze

e Storiche (Milano), vol. 53 (1920), 539-549.

W. Jaeger, *Aristoteles: Eine Geschichte seiner Ent-
    wicklung* (1st edit., 1923, 2nd edit. 1955, English
    translation, 2nd edit., 1948).

H. Gadamer, "Der Aristotelische Protreptikos und die
    Entwicklungsgeschichtliche Betrachtung der Ar-
    istotelischen Ethik," *Hermes*, vol. 63 (1928), 138-
    165.

M. Needler, "The Aristotelian *Protrepticus* and the
    Developmental Treatment of the Aristotelian Eth-
    ics," *Classical Philology*, vol. 23 (1928), 280-284.

B. Einarson, "Aristotle's *Protrepticus* and the Struc-
    ture of the *Epinomis*," *Transactions and Proceed-
    ings of the American Philological Association*
    (Ithaca, N.Y., 1936), 261-285.

P. Von der Mühll, "Isokrates und der Protreptikos des
    Aristoteles," *Philologus*, vol. 94 (1939/40), 259-
    265.

I. Düring, "Problems in Aristotle's Protrepticus,"
    Eranos, vol. 52 (1954), 139-171.

W. G. Rabinowitz, *Aristotle's Protrepticus and the
    Sources of its Reconstruction* (Univ. of Calif.
    Publications in Classical Philology, vol. 16, 1957).

A. D. Leeman, "De Aristotelis Protreptico Somnii
    Scipionis exemplo," *Mnemosyne*, vol. 11 (1958),
    139-151

G. Zuntz, "In Aristotelis Protrepticum Coniecturae,"
    Mnemosyne, vol. 11 (1958), 158-159.

S. Mansion, "Contemplation and Action in Aristotle's
    Protrepticus," in: *Aristotle and Plato in the Mid-
    Fourth Century* (edit. I. Düring and G. E. L.
    Owen, 1960), pp. 56-75.

É. de Strycker, "On the First Section of Frag. 5 of the
    Protrepticus," in: *Aristotle and Plato in the Mid-
    Fourth Century*, pp. 76-104.

I. Düring, *Aristotle's Protrepticus*: *An Attempt at Reconstruction* (Studia Graeca et Latina Gothoburgensia, vol. 12, 1961).

E. Berti, *La Filosofia del Primo Aristotele* (Università di Padova Pubblicazioni della Facultà di Lettere e Filosofia, vol. 38, 1962) pp. 453-543.

Protrepticus

The Text

(Fragments enclosed by brackets are of doubtful authenticity.)

— 1 —

[The *Protrepticus* of Aristotle was addressed to
Themison, king of Cyprus. In it Aristotle maintained
that no man had more earthly goods than Themison
for devoting his life to philosophy. For Themison possessed great wealth and, hence, could not only spend
money on this endeavor, but also could lend his re-
nown to this task.]

— 2 —

[Preoccupation with worldly goods] may prevent
men from doing what they regard to be their duty.
But when we perceive the plight of these men, we
most certainly ought to resolve to avoid these worldly
goods by insisting that true happiness consists neither
in the acquisition of much wealth nor in the particular
disposition of the soul. No one could possibly claim
that the body is happy simply because it is draped
in gorgeous garments. It is happy because it is healthy
and well disciplined, even if it possesses none of the
things we have mentioned. By the same token, if

the soul is educated and disciplined, such a soul and
such a man ought to be called happy. This is certainly not true, however, of the man who is endowed
with many worldly goods, but who himself is without
worth. For although it may have golden curb-chains
and an expensive harness, we do not value a horse
afflicted with an ugly disposition, but rather the one
that is well disciplined.

— 3 —

In addition, whenever worthless men attain to great
wealth, they tend to value this wealth more highly
than the goods or virtues of the soul. But this is the
worst of all possible conditions. For just as a man is
universally held in contempt if he be inferior to his
own servants, so too are those who consider worldly
possessions of greater importance than their own natures.

— 4 —

Indeed, this is so: surfeit, as the saying goes, begets
insolence (or, wantonness); and lack of erudition,
when allied with power, results in folly. Neither
wealth nor strength nor beauty is of much use to
those who have an evil and ill-disposed soul. The
more lavishly a man is endowed with these things,
the more serious and frequent harm they cause to
him who possesses them but, at the same time, lacks
true wisdom (*phronesis*). The popular saying, "no
knife for a child," signifies here: "No power should
ever be given to mean men."

— 5 —

All men are in agreement that true wisdom (*phronesis*) comes from learning, and from the pursuit of those things which philosophy enables us to pursue. This being so, we must most assuredly pursue philosophy without fear or reproach and . . . (?).

— 6 —

The term "to philosophize" (or, "to pursue philosophy") implies two distinct things: first, whether or not we ought to seek [after philosophic truth] at all; and, second, our dedication to philosophic speculation (*philosophon theoria*).

— 7 —

[Since we are addressing ourselves to human beings rather than to divine beings, we must include in these exhortations such advice as is of use in political and practical life. Let us now begin the discussion of these matters.]

— 8 —

[The things with which we are equipped for this life and which pertain to this life, such as the body and certain other things that belong to the body, are given to us as tools. The use of these tools is always fraught with danger. Moreover, those who do not use them properly (or wisely) experience a great many unexpected effects. We ought to endeavor, therefore, not only to acquire but also to use properly that kind

of knowledge which enables us to make the best use
of all these tools. Hence, if we are to govern people
rightly and live our own lives usefully and fittingly,
we must become philosophers.]

— 9 —

[Indeed, there exist different kinds of knowledge:
some kinds of knowledge produce the good things in
life, while others make use of these first kinds of knowledge. Some kinds of knowledge are ancillary, while
others are prescriptive. The prescriptive kinds, which
at the same time are more authoritative, are most
closely related to the true (or ultimate) good. If,
therefore, only that kind of knowledge which brings
about the correctness of judgment — which, in other
words, makes use of reason and aims at the good as
a whole — in brief, if only philosophy is in a position
to make the proper use of all other kinds of knowledge and to steer them in accordance with the principles of nature (or reality), then we ought to strive
incessantly and in every possible way to become philosophers. Because philosophy, and philosophy alone,
comprises right judgment and unerring wisdom, it
commands what ought and ought not to be done.]

— 10 —

Of all things that come into being, some originate
either from some thought or from some art, such as,
for instance, a house or a ship (for the cause of both
of these is a certain art and a definite way of reasoning). Others, again, come into being not at all by way

of art, but by nature. Nature is the cause of animals
and plants, and all such things come into being according to nature. But some things, again, also come
into being as the result of chance. And we say of most
of the things that come into being neither by art,
nature, nor necessity, that they come into being by
chance.

— 11 —

Now of the things that come into being by chance,
none comes into being on account of, nor has, any
particular purpose. But those things that come into
being by art have an end as well as a purpose (for he
who masters an art will tell you the reason why he
wrote and for what purpose he did so). And a thing
that comes into being for some other purpose is better than that which comes into being for its own
sake. I speak here of things whose cause, in keeping
with their nature, is art rather than chance. For we
ought to call the art of medicine more appropriately
the art of making people healthy than the art of
making people sick, and architecture the art of build-
ing houses rather than of tearing them down. Hence,
everything that is by art comes into being for a purpose, and this is its best feature as well as its best
end. But whatever comes into being by chance, comes
into being without a purpose. Now something good
might come into being by chance. Yet, in respect of
chance and to the extent that it is the product of
chance, it is not good. Because that which comes into
being by chance is always indeterminate and indefi-
nite.

– 12 –

All that comes into being according to nature, however, also comes into being for a purpose, and furthermore, comes into being for a superior purpose to
that which comes into being through art. For nature
does not imitate art, but art, rather, imitates nature.
Art exists to assist nature and to complete what nature leaves undone. Certain things nature seems to be
able to complete by herself unassisted, while other
things she can complete only with difficulty or not at
all. An example close at hand is the process by which
things come into being: some seeds, it will be noticed,
germinate without protection, no matter what ground
they fall on; others, however, stand in need of the
art of farming as well. In like manner, some animals
attain to their full nature by themselves, while man
requires many arts for his survival, not only at birth
but also in matters of subsequent growth.

– 13 –

If, therefore, art imitates nature, it is to nature that
the arts owe the fact that all of their productions come
into being for an end. For we must surmise that everything that comes into being properly comes into being
for an end: that which turns out to be good and
beautiful comes into being properly, and everything
that comes into being or has come into being, provided it did so according to nature, turns out to be
beautiful [and good], especially since that which is
contrary to nature is bad and [contrary to that which
is] according to nature. Coming into being [according
to nature, therefore,] is always for an end.

— 14 —

This can be observed in any one part of our bodies: if, for instance, you consider the eyelid, you will notice that it has come into being, not at random, but to assist the eye by giving it rest and by protecting it against objects that might strike it. And we mean the same thing when we assert that something has come into being [by nature] for an end, and that [the product of art] ought to have come into being for a purpose. If, for example, a ship ought to be built in order to provide transportation by sea, it is for this reason [or purpose] that it has come into being.

— 15 —

Now either all of the animals, or at least the best and worthiest of them, belong to the class of things that have come into being by nature [and according to nature]. And it makes no difference if some people should be of the opinion that most of the animals have come into being contrary to nature, that is, in order to wreak havoc and cause mischief. The worthiest of all animals on earth is man. This should indicate beyond all doubt that he has come into being by nature and according to nature [and, hence, for a purpose].

— 16 —

At this point we may ask the question: since we are distinguished from all other existing things, for what particular purpose have nature and God brought us into being? Pythagoras, when asked this question,

replied: "To view (or, contemplate) the heavens."
And he added that he was a viewer of nature, and
had come into life for this purpose.

— 17 —

And when people inquired of Anaxagoras for what
purpose one should decide to come into being and
for what purpose one should live, he is reported to
have answered: "To view (or, contemplate) whatever pertains to the heavens and to the stars and the
moon and the sun in the heavens, everything else
being of no importance."

— 18 —

If, then, the end to which each thing is ordained
is always superior to the thing itself (for everything
that comes into being does so for a particular end,
and the ultimate end is better and, as a matter of
fact, the best of all things); and if by "end according
to nature" we mean "that which is perfected last" in
the process of generation, at least as long as this process of generation is continuous; and if, in addition, we
concede that the component parts of men's bodies
are completed or perfected, first, the mental parts
later, and that the completion or perfection of the
better is somehow always later than its generation;
and if we concede that the soul is later than the
body and that wisdom comes last to the soul — for
we all realize that by its very nature wisdom is the last
to come into being for men (and this is the reason
why old age claims wisdom alone of all good things)

— if all this is true, then some form of wisdom is (by nature) our end, and the practice of wisdom is the ultimate activity. And for the sake of this activity [i.e., for the practice of wisdom] we have come into being. For we must concede that if we have come into being in order to practice wisdom and to acquire knowledge, then we also exist for that end.

— 19 —

According to this argument, then, Pythagoras was correct in maintaining that every man has been created by God to acquire knowledge and to contemplate. But it will be considered later whether the object of this knowledge is the universe or some other nature. What we have stated so far suffices as a first conclusion. For if wisdom is our end according to nature, the practice of wisdom must be the best of all things.

— 20 —

Hence, we should do all other things for the sake of the goods that reside in man himself, and of these, that which is good in the body we should do for the sake of that which is good in the soul. And we ought to practice virtue for the sake of wisdom, because wisdom is the supreme end.

— 21 —

[Since nature is endowed with reason, no matter what form she assumes, she does nothing haphazardly, but always and everywhere acts for an end. Rejecting chance, she is concerned about the end more than are the arts, especially since the arts are but imitations of nature. Since man is by nature composed of soul and body, and since the soul is better than the body, and since that which is inferior is always the servant of that which is superior, the body must exist for the sake of the soul. And inasmuch as the soul consists of a rational part and an irrational part, the latter being the inferior part, we must conclude that the irrational part exists for the sake of the rational part. And since reason belongs to the rational part of the soul, the above demonstration forces us to assert that everything exists for the sake of reason.]

— 22 —

[The activity most appropriate to reason is thinking, and thinking (*noesis*) is the visualization of intelligible things, just as the perception of visible things is the activity of sight. Thought and reason, therefore, are what make everything else desirable for men. Other things, that is, things outside the soul, are, to be sure, desirable for the sake of the soul. But reason is the superior part of the soul, and these other things, as we have seen, exist for the sake of what is superior.]

— 23 —

[Furthermore, of all thoughts only those are free or 'liberal' which are entertained for their own sake. But those thoughts which produce knowledge for the sake of something else are like female slaves (?). A thing pursued as an end in itself is always superior to one that is pursued merely as a means to something else. And, as it is universally held, that which is free is always superior to that which is not free.]

— 24 —

[If in our actions we use our intellect, even though in so acting we take into consideration our own advantage and adjust our actions to this consideration, yet we are guided by our intellect. We use our bodies as servants, and in so doing we may also be victims of chance. But as a rule we perform those actions well in which reason dominates, even if most actions are performed through the instrumentality of the body.]

— 25 —

[Thinking and speculation for their own sake, then, are more honorable than, and superior to, thinking and speculation directed to securing some advantage. Pure speculation in itself is honorable, and wisdom of the intellectual type among the various modes of thinking is certainly the most exalted, just as wisdom combined with practical insight is the most exalted among all intellectual activites concerned with the purpose of action. The good and the honorable, then, are to be discovered, above all, in pure philosophic speculation. Not every kind of pure speculation, however, is honorable (in an absolute sense), but only that which originates in an absolute mind and, again, that which is pure speculation or contemplation of

the first or ruling principle of the universe. This kind
of pure speculation is intimately associated with philosophical wisdom, and it may be properly maintained
that this is wisdom in the true sense of the term.]

— 26 —

[Devoid of sense and reason, man becomes like a
plant; deprived of reason alone, he turns into a wild
beast; but rising above irrationality by relying on reason, he becomes like God.]

— 27 —

[For that which distinguishes us from all other animals shines forth in a life lived according to reason
— a life in which nothing happens according to blind
chance, a life which has no truck with petty concerns. Animals have a small spark of rationality and
a modicum of intelligence, but they are totally devoid
of philosophic (theoretical) wisdom [which is the
exclusive prerogative of the gods]. But as to sense
perception and instinct, man has less acuteness and
less physical strength than many animals.]

— 28 —

[This (*scil.*, life according to reason) cannot possibly be divorced from the good. As a matter of fact, we
are forced to concede that it is implied in the notion
of the good. For the good man who lives a life according to reason never subjects himself to chance,
but more than any other man rises above the things

that happen by chance. Hence, if you embrace wholeheartedly a life according to reason, you have every
reason to be confident and of good cheer.]

— 29 —

Moreover, since every man chooses what he is
capable of doing as well as what is advantageous to
him, we must concede that these two problems are
closely related to philosophy. But we must also admit
that, although we are all more inclined to do what is
easy, nevertheless the difficulty connected with the
acquisition of philosophic training is more than com-
pensated for by its usefulness.

— 30 —

It is easy to demonstrate that we are capable of
acquiring the sciences concerned with what is just
and what is expedient as well as those concerned
with nature and the other aspects of truth.

— 31 —

For, the prior is always more knowable than the
posterior, and the "better by nature" is more knowable than the worse. For rational knowledge is more
concerned with what is defined and ordered than
with its contraries, and more with causes than with
effects. Now, good things are more defined and ordered than evil things, and since this is also true of
men, a good man is better defined and more ordered

than an evil man. In addition, things that are prior
are causes, more so than things that are posterior.
For if the former are removed, the things that derive their being from them also are removed: length,
if numbers are removed; planes, if length is removed;
solids, if planes are removed; and syllables, if letters
are removed.

— 32 —

Hence, if the soul (being by nature abler to com-
mand) is superior to the body, and if there are arts
and sciences concerned with the body, such as medicine or gymnastics (for we consider these as sciences
and say that some people master them), clearly,
then, there exists, regarding the soul and its faculties
and virtues, a scientific concern as well as an art which
we can acquire, the more so, since we can achieve
this even with regard to things concerning which our
ignorance is greater and the knowledge of which
is more difficult to acquire.

— 33 —

This also holds true in regard to matters concerning nature: it is of far greater necessity, as a matter
of fact, of first necessity, to have a knowledge of
causes and of the first elements, rather than, perhaps,
of things dependent on them. For the latter do not
belong to the highest order (of reality), nor do the
first principles arise from them. It is only from and
through the first principles that all other things de-
monstrably proceed and are constituted.

— 34 —

Whether it be fire, or air, or number, or any of
the other natures that constitute the causes and first
principles of all other things, as long as we are ignorant of these causes and first principles, we cannot
know any of the other things. For how could we
possibly recognize speech if we did not know the
syllables, or know syllables if we knew none of the
letters?

— 35 —

For the time being, however, let us be satisfied
with what we have said so far about our subject,
namely, that there is a science of truth as well as a
science of the excellence of the soul.

— 36 —

From what is to follow it will become evident
that philosophic wisdom (*phronesis*) is the greatest
of all goods, and, at the same time, the most useful
of all things. We all agree that the best man, the man
who by nature has the greatest moral strength, ought
to rule. And we also agree that the law alone should
be the ruler, the ultimate authority — but only a law
which not only contains the language of wisdom and
reason, but also manifests wisdom and reason.

— 37 —

But then, what more accurate standard of, what
more competent guide to goodness do we have than

the man who possesses philosophic wisdom? For whatever course of action such a man may choose, his choice, provided it is dictated by his knowledge, will be good, and its opposite bad.

— 38 —

Since by mere preference all men choose what accords most with their own nature or character (the just man choosing to live justly, the brave man to live bravely, and the temperate man to live temperately), by the same token the wise man will choose, above all, to use his wisdom and his intellect wisely, the more so since this constitutes the proper exercise of his particular faculty or powers. It is obvious, therefore, that according to the most authoritative opinion, philosophic wisdom (*phronesis*) is the greatest of all goods.

— 39 —

The truth of what has just been said should become even more obvious from the following: to think rationally and wisely, and to acquire rational knowledge, in itself is not only desirable for men (because it is impossible to live a life worthy of man without these), but also useful for practical life. For unless something is accomplished after we have formed a rational judgment about it and acted in accordance with this rational judgment, no real good will accrue to us. [But irrespective of whether to live a good life depends on worldly possessions or on being virtuous or on possessing wisdom (*phronesis*), we ought to pursue philosophy always and everywhere. Because it is above all through the active practice of philosophy that we arrive at clear notions about these matters.]

— 40 —

But to seek from every form of knowledge something other than knowledge itself, and to expect that knowledge as such must always be useful in a practical sense, are simply the expectations of a man who is totally ignorant of the basic discrepancy separating (philosophically) good things from practically necessary things. For these two stand at opposite extremes. Of those things without which life is impossible, those which are desired for the sake of something else are to be called practical necessities and secondary or ancillary causes. But those things which are desired for their own sake, even should nothing else (no immediate practical effect) result from them, ought to be called "good" in the highest sense of the term. For this is not desirable or desired for the sake of that, and that again for the sake of something else, and so *ad infinitum*. There must be a terminal point to this somewhere. It is ridiculous, indeed, to expect from everything some kind of benefit beyond the thing itself, and to ask, 'What do we gain by it?' or, 'Of what use is it?' The truth is, as we insist, that he who asks such questions is certainly not one who knows and understands the beautiful and the good, or one who can distinguish between first causes and secondary causes.

— 41 —

The truth of what we have been saying would be
seen most clearly if someone would carry us in spirit
to the Islands of the Blessed. There we would not
stand in need of anything or perhaps expect some advantage from anything, for there everything has been
left behind except the intellectual life and philosophic speculation. This is a condition which even in
this world we call the truly free life. If this is true,
would not anyone of us justifiably feel ashamed if,
given the opportunity to dwell on the Islands of the
Blessed, he would by his own default fail to do so?
The reward, therefore, that comes to men from philosophic knowledge is not to be despised, nor should the
good that is derived from it be taken lightly. The
wise men among the ancient poets long ago pointed
out that we shall receive our just deserts in Hades.
By the same token, it is plausible that we should
receive the gifts of philosophic wisdom (*phronesis*)
in the Islands of the Blessed.

— 42 —

Hence, it is by no means strange that philosophic
wisdom should appear devoid of immediate practical usefulness and, at the same time, not prove itself
advantageous. For we call it not advantageous but
good, and it ought to be pursued, not for the sake of
anything else, but for its own sake. For, as we
journey to the games at Olympia for the sake of the
spectacle itself, even if we derive from it nothing
more tangible than the sight of the spectacle itself
(for the spectacle itself is worth more than 'much

money'); and as we watch the Dionysia not in order to derive some profit from the actors — as a matter of fact, we spend money on them; and as there are many more spectacles we ought to prefer to great riches, so, too, the viewing and contemplation of the universe is to be valued above all things considered to be useful in a practical sense. For, most certainly, it would make little sense were we to take pains to watch men imitating women and slaves, or fighting or running, but not think it proper to view, free of all charge, the nature and the true reality of everything that is.

— 43 —

From the arts and professions (crafts) it can readily be seen that theoretical (or philosophic) knowledge (*phronesis*) is of the greatest use to us in managing our practical lives. Just as all the outstanding members of the medical profession and the majority of those who are experts in physical training agree that those who are planning to be good physicians and good coaches must have a general acquaintance with nature, so, too, must good lawgivers have an all-encompassing knowledge of nature — and as a matter of fact, a better knowledge and understanding of nature than the physicians or coaches. For the former use their skill exclusively for the sake of the well-being and strength of the human body, but the latter, being concerned not only with the well-being and virtues of the soul, but also with teaching the salvation and perdition of the whole commonweal, need philosophy to an even greater degree.

— 44 —

For, in general or ordinary crafts and craftsmanlike operations, the most efficient tools are directly derived from nature — for instance, the carpenter's rule, rod, or compass in the builder's trade — since we derive some of our tools from observing the behavior of water, other tools from observing the behavior of light and of sun rays. And it is through our reliance on these tools that we determine what, according to our senses, is sufficiently straight and smooth. So, then, in the same manner, the statesman must have some definite standards derived from nature as well as from truth (or, reality) itself, by which he will determine what is just, what is good, and what is expedient. For just as in the general or ordinary crafts the above-mentioned tools are superior to all other tools, so, too, the most excellent standards or basic norms are those which are established in the greatest possible conformity with nature (or reality).

— 45 —

But no one, who has not practiced philosophy (and is capable of practicing philosophy) and has not learned (objective) truth, will be capable of doing this. Also, in the general or ordinary arts or crafts men do not, perhaps, derive their tools and their most minute reckoning from first principles, and thus achieve something close to scientific knowledge: rather, they borrow them at second, third, or even more remote hand, and base their reasoning on empirical observations. The philosopher alone, of all men, imitates that

which among all things is the most exact; for, what
he looks at is originality and exactness itself, not
merely imitation.

— 46 —

And so, just as a house-builder who borrows his
measurements from other buildings instead of using
the rod and other technical instruments is not a good
architect, thus, similarly, one who either enacts laws
for cities or administers public affairs by observing and
imitating the public administrations or constitutions
devised by other men, whether those of the Lacedae-
monians, Cretans, or any other commonwealth, is not
a good lawgiver or a conscientious statesman. For an
imitation of that which is not good in itself cannot
possibly be good, nor can an imitation of what in its
nature is not divine (imperishable) and stable, be
imperishable and stable. It is obvious, however, that
among all craftsmen the philosopher alone is familiar
with laws that are truly stable and with practices
that are both truly right and truly proper.

— 47 —

For, the philosopher, and he alone, lives with his
gaze fixed on nature (reality) and on the divine
(imperishable); and like a good helmsman [who takes
his bearings from the stars] he will try to tie his life
to what is eternal and unchanging, moor it to first
principles, and, hence, will live as the master of his
own [soul].

— 48 —

Admittedly, this kind of knowledge is purely theoretical. Nevertheless, it enables us to determine our
whole practical conduct and all our practical actions
in accordance with this knowledge. For, just as sight
in itself produces or creates nothing (its only assign-
ment being to distinguish and to reveal to us all that
can physically be seen), yet it not only enables us to
act as it directs but also assists us greatly in all our
actions (for without sight we would be almost completely immobilized), so it is also evident that, although rational knowledge is purely theoretical, we
still perform thousands of things in full conformity
with rational (theoretical) knowledge, and, in fact,
decide upon certain actions and forego others. Thus,
on account of reason (and theoretical knowledge),
we achieve everything that is called good.

— 49 —

[He who inquires into these matters ought, however, never to overlook the fact that the goodness inherent in all the things that are good and useful to
human life depends on use and practice, and not on
theoretical knowledge alone. We improve our health
not merely by knowing what makes us healthy but
by actually applying this knowledge to our bodies.
By the same token, we become wealthy not merely
by knowing what constitutes wealth, but by actually
acquiring and possessing much property. And most
important of all, we live well not merely by knowing
something about reality, but by acting properly, that
is, in accordance with this reality. For this is truly

well-being. From all this it follows that philosophy, too, if it is to be useful, must be either the doing of good things or something of use as a means of producing good acts.]

— 50 —

Hence, we ought not to avoid philosophy, particularly if, as we believe, philosophy is the acquisition and exercise of wisdom, and wisdom is among the greatest of goods. And if, in the pursuit of material gain, we assume many risks by sailing to the very pillars of Hercules, we certainly should not spare any labor or expense in the pursuit of philosophic wisdom (*phronesis*). It is characteristic of the brutish man to desire life rather than to strive after the good life, to listen to the opinions of the many rather than to expect the many to listen to his own opinions, and to seek after money rather than to do something about acquiring what is truly exalted.

— 51 —

As regards the value and greatness of our subject matter, I believe we have proved our case. That the acquisition of wisdom is really much easier than the acquisition of other goods may convincingly be shown by the following arguments.

— 52 —

People who pursue philosophy do not get any reward from their fellow men and, hence, receive no

incentive for the efforts they make. They may have
spent much (money, time and effort) on the acquisition of other skills and arts, yet in a short span of
time their progress in exact knowledge is rapid. This
seems to me to be an indication of how easy philosophy actually is.

— 53 —

Also, the fact that all men feel at ease in philosophy,
wishing to dedicate their whole lives to the pursuit of
it by leaving behind all other concerns, is in itself
weighty evidence that it is a painless pleasure to
dedicate oneself wholeheartedly to philosophy. For
no one is willing to engage in exhausting work for a
long time. In addition, a preoccupation with philosophy differs most radically from all other occupations.
Those who are engaged in philosophy need neither
special tools nor a particular workshop for what they
are doing. For wherever in the whole world one puts
one's mind to work, one is able to take hold of the
truth as if it were in fact omnipresent.

— 54 —

In this fashion, it has been demonstrated that philosophy is not only possible, but that it is also the
greatest of goods and fairly easy to acquire. Hence,
for the sake of all this, it is most worthwhile that we
should enthusiastically take hold of it.

— 55 —

Again, part of us is soul, part body; one rules while

the other is ruled; one makes use of the other, while the other functions as an instrument. Furthermore, the use made of that which is ruled is always coordinated with that which rules and uses.

— 56 —

To the soul there belongs, on the one hand, reason (which rules according to nature and decides matters concerning ourselves), and, on the other hand, that which is, so to speak, in attendance, and which according to its nature ought to be ruled. Everything is in perfect order if everything performs according to its proper function; and the achievement of this perfect order is in itself a good.

— 57 —

As a matter of fact, when the best, the most authoritative and the most honored parts of the soul hold a foremost or dominant position, then we have the perfect order. In the natural hierarchy of values, that which is by nature superior should hold a superior position. And that which is by nature more qualified to rule and more authoritative is always superior, just as man is superior to all other animals. This being so, the soul is superior to, and better than, the body (for it is more qualified to rule), and of the soul itself, that part which has reason and the power to reason is the better part. For, that which commands and indicates what we ought and ought not to do is superior and better.

— 58 —

Whatever the superiority or excellence of this part
of the soul may be, this superiority must be the most
desirable of all things, not only for all creatures in
general, but for us in particular. For one might maintain, I believe, that this part is, either alone or to a
greater degree than anything else, our true self.

— 59 —

Furthermore, when a thing accomplishes in the
best possible way what it is supposed to accomplish
and does so not by sheer accident but by its own
nature, then that thing must be called "the best";
and that excellence by virtue of which each thing is
capable of achieving this result must be called its
most exalted excellence.

— 60 —

Now that which is composite and divisible into
many parts has many and different functions. But
that which by nature is simple and whose being does
not consist merely with reference to something else,
this must of necessity have one single overriding excellence.

— 61 —

If, therefore, man is a simple noncomposite living
being, and if his being and essence are determined
in accordance with reason and intelligence, then he
has no other function or ordination than the attain-

ment of the most exact truth which is the truth about reality. But, if he is a composite being made up of several faculties or powers, then it is clear that in such a case, to wit, when someone is capable of performing several functions, the most outstanding of his several functions and powers always constitutes his most appropriate work or concern: health, for instance, is the physician's most appropriate concern, and safety that of the pilot. Now we can name no better work or concern more appropriate to the intellect or intellectual part of the soul than the attainment of truth. Hence, truth is the most exalted and most appropriate concern and work of the rational part of the soul.

— 62 —

Obviously, the soul accomplishes its foremost task by acquiring rational knowledge or, to be more exact, by acquiring a higher and more perfect form of knowledge. And the highest, as well as most compelling, purpose underlying all this is the understanding and knowledge of truth and reality (*theoria*). For whenever one of two things is chosen for the sake of the other, then the latter is better than, superior to, and preferable to the former: for instance, pleasure is better than and preferable to pleasant things, and health better than and preferable to wholesome things. For the latter are, so to speak, productive of the former.

— 63 —

Now, if we were to compare one faculty of the

soul with another, there is nothing preferable to rational insight and philosophic wisdom (*phronesis*), that is, to that faculty which is actually a controlling power within us. For the rational part of the soul, whether by itself or in relation to the other parts, is better than and superior to all the rest of the soul, and its excellence consists in rational knowledge.

— 64 —

Hence, none of the so-called specific virtues or faculties (or powers) is the proper function or domain of this rational part of the soul, for the rational part is better than, and superior to, all of the other parts. The end achieved is always better than and superior to the knowledge or technique productive of this end. And neither is every excellence (virtue or power) nor happiness of the soul, thus conceived, always the product of philosophic insight. For if philosophic insight is to be creative, it will have to produce something different from itself. Thus, for instance, the art (or technique) of house-building produces a house, but it is not part of a house. But rational insight (*phronesis*) is part of the excellence of the soul as well as of its happiness. For we maintain that true happiness either stems from rational insight (*phronesis*), or is this rational insight itself.

— 65 —

According to this argument, philosophic (or rational) insight (*phronesis*) cannot be practical (or productive) knowledge, since the end must be better than that which tries to attain it. Now nothing is better than or superior to philosophic insight (*phronesis*), unless it be one of the things we have mentioned. But none of these things is really a function different from philosophic insight. Hence, it must be admitted that this sort of knowledge (*episteme*) is purely theoretical (or speculative), inasmuch as it is impossible to see how its end is actually to create something.

— 66 —

From all this it follows that philosophic speculation (*theorein*) and philosophic contemplation are the proper functions of the soul, and that the philosophic speculation is of all things the most desirable activity of men, comparable, I submit, to sight. For one would prefer to have sight, even though nothing but vision were to result from it.

— 67 —

Furthermore, if we cherish one thing because something else necessarily results from it, surely we shall wish more for that which produces the desired result to a fuller extent. Thus, if a man likes to walk because he is healthy, but discovers that running is even more conducive to health and that he can achieve health through running (and that he is able to run), he will prefer to run, and, if he knows this (that running is better than walking), will rather run than walk. If, therefore, true opinion (*doxa*) is similar to philosophic insight (*phronesis*) — and it is admitted here that

true opinion, because it is true, may properly be
chosen to the extent and manner to which it is akin
to philosophic insight — then philosophic insight is
still preferable to true opinion for the simple reason
that the attainment of truth is achieved to a greater
degree by philosophic insight.

— 68 —

Again, if we love sight for its own sake, this alone
should be sufficient evidence that all men love thinking and knowing above everything else.

— 69 —

But living, indeed, is distinguished from non-living
by sense-perception, and we define life as the actuality as well as the faculty of using sense-perception.
If this is taken away, life is not worth living: it is as
though through the loss of sense-perception life itself were taken away.

— 70 —

Now among all sense-perceptions, the faculty of
sight is distinguished in that it is the clearest of all,
and it is on this account that we prefer sight to all
other senses. But the faculty of every sense to acquire
knowledge operates through the body, as, for instance,
hearing perceives sound by means of the ears.

— 71 —

Hence, if life is preferred and valued on account

of sense-perception, and if sense-perception is a sort of knowledge, and if, further, on account of this or through this the soul is in a position to know, then it is for this [ability to know] that we want to live.

— 72 —

In addition, if, as we have just pointed out, the more preferable of two things is always that which possesses the desirable quality to a greater degree, then, of necessity, sight must be the most preferable and the most excellent of the several senses. But philosophic insight (*phronesis*), because it has a stronger hold on truth, is preferable to mere physical sight and to all other senses, and even to life itself. And this is the reason why all men strive after knowledge above all.

— 73 —

Because in loving life, they love thinking and knowing; they love life for no other reason than for the sake of experiencing life, and, above all, for the sake of sight. Apparently, they love this faculty above everything else, because, in comparison with all other senses, sight is simply a sort of knowledge.

— 74 —

From the argument which follows, it will become clear that those who have decided upon a life according to reason are also those who enjoy life most.

— 75 —

The expression "to live" apparently is used in two
different ways: one implies a potentiality, the other
an actuality. For we describe as beings endowed with
sight not only those animals which have sight and
are born able to see, even though they happened to
have their eyes shut, but also those animals which
are using this faculty by looking at something. The
situation is similar with the faculty of knowing and
understanding: here we mean by it sometimes the
faculty as well as the actual process of thinking, sometimes the possession of this faculty as well as the possession of knowledge.

— 76 —

If, then, we distinguish "to live" from "not to live"
by the criterion of "being able to have sense perception" — and this "being able to have sense perception"
again has two meanings, signifying above all "to make
use of one's senses," but in another way meaning "to
be able to use one's senses" (this being the reason, it
seems, why we say that even a sleeping man has
perceptions) — then it will be clear, in accordance
with what has just been said, that the expression "to
live" must have two separate meanings: for of a waking man it will have to be said that he lives in the
true and proper sense of the term, while of a sleeping man it must be said that he lives because he is
able to change to that kind of activity in reference
to which we say that a man is awake and perceiving
certain things. It is for this reason, and with reference
to what has just been pointed out, [that we must call
him "alive."]

— 77 —

Hence, whenever we use the same term in two different senses, the one signifying action, the other potentiality, we define the former as expressing the more concise meaning of the term. For instance, we use the term "to know" with reference to a person who is actually using his faculty to know as well as his knowledge, rather than with reference to a person who merely possesses knowledge; and the term "to see," likewise, with reference to a person who is actually looking at something, rather than with reference to a person who merely is able to look at something.

— 78 —

And we use the term "more" in connection with things for which there is only one designation — and the term "more" signifies here not only "to a greater degree," but also [a logical or axiological] priority. Thus we say, for instance, that health is "more" of a good than wholesome things. And similarly, we insist that that which by its own nature is preferable as a choice is "more" of a good than that which is productive of this choice. Nevertheless, we notice that the same term "good" is predicated to both, although not in its absolute sense. For we say of useful things as well as of things which are in themselves excellent that they are "good."

— 79 —

Hence, we must say that a waking man "lives more" than a sleeping man, and that a man who is exercising

his mental gifts "lives more" than a man who merely
possesses mental gifts. And it is on account of the
former that we maintain that the latter "lives." Because living man is so constituted that he can be
either passive or active [as regards the use of his
natural endowments].

— 80 —

The practice of anything, therefore, is this: if something can be done only one way, it is done when
one does just that thing. If it can be done in more
than one way, it is done when one does it the best
possible way; for instance, when someone plays the
flute, he either just plays it, whenever he uses it, or
he plays it the best possible way. And we use the
same argument as regards other activities. Thus we
must concede that he who does a thing rightly "does
it more" (or, "better"), for he who does something
well and painstakingly has a purpose and does in a
natural way whatever he does.

— 81 —

It has previously been stated that thinking and
reasoning, either by themselves or above everything
else, are activities (or the work) of the soul. In view
of what has been said previously, it is a simple inference, which can easily be drawn by everyone, that
the man who thinks correctly in a certain sense "lives
more" and more excellently than others; and that he
who attains to the highest form or degree of truth
likewise lives to the highest degree. For this is the

man who thinks and speculates in terms of the most
precise knowledge. It is to this kind of man that the
most perfect life belongs, namely, to those who reason and to those who have intellectual insight.

— 82 —

Now, if living as such is for every animal its true
being, then it becomes evident that the thinking and
rational animal has being in the highest degree and
in the most compelling sense, and most of all if it
uses this faculty or power in the contemplation of
what is most knowable of all things.

— 83 —

Moreover, the perfect activity that is not impeded
or interfered with [from the outside] contains delights
in itself. Hence, the activity of the intellect must be
the most delightful of all activites.

— 84 —

Furthermore, there is a difference between enjoying
oneself while drinking and enjoying drinking as such.
For there is nothing to prevent a man, who is neither
thirsty nor getting the particular drink he enjoys,
from enjoying himself while drinking, and this not
perchance because he is drinking but because he happens at the same time to be looking at something
[while drinking] or to be looked at, as he sits down to
drink. Thus, we may say that such a man enjoys
himself and, as a matter of fact, enjoys himself while

drinking, but not because he is drinking or, perhaps, that he enjoys drinking as such. By the same token we can maintain that walking, sitting down, learning, or, for that matter, any activity, is either pleasant or painful, but not because we happen to experience pain or pleasure in the presence of these activities, but because we are all pained or pleased by their presence.

— 85 —

Similarly, we call that kind of life pleasant whose presence is pleasant to those who live it; and we insist that not all men who experience pleasures while living enjoy life, but merely those to whom life itself is pleasant and who delight in the pleasure that comes from being alive.

— 86 —

It is for this reason that we declare the man who is awake, rather than the man who is asleep, "to be living" and "to be alive" — the man who thinks, rather than the man who is without thought. And we also insist that the delight of living is that kind of pleasure which we derive from the activities of the soul. For this is the true life.

— 87 —

If, then, there is more than just one disciplined activity of the soul, the act of thinking is and ought to be the controlling force of all the activities of the soul as far as possible. Hence, it is obvious that of necessity the delight derived from thinking and intellectual contemplation, alone or most of all, consists in the pleasure of living. A pleasant life and the capacity for true enjoyment, therefore, belong only or most of all to intellectual men who are thinking. For the activity of our thoughts and of our intellect which is most true in that it is stimulated by the most real of all realities — particularly if it preserves forever and without wavering the perfection which it receives — generates more delight than all other activities.

— 88 —

[Thus the capacity for enjoying good and true pleasures in itself is a good reason why intelligent men should practice philosophy.]

— 89 —

[We will reach the same conclusion] not merely by summing up the several parts or elements that constitute happiness, but also by penetrating this problem more deeply and by considering happiness as a whole. Hence, we may state explicitly that, as dedication to philosophy is related to happiness, so also it underlies the very criterion which determines whether we are good men or evil men. For all things that are worthwhile are so because they are either conducive to or the result of true happiness. And of the several parts or elements that make up happiness some are necessary and others just pleasant.

— 90 —

It is for this very reason that we define happiness
either as a kind of intellectual activity (*phronesis*)
and as a sort of wisdom (*sophia*), or as the foremost
possession as well as the perfect practice of "virtue,"
or as all these.

— 91 —

Now, if true happiness is first of all intellectual
activity or wisdom, then it should be obvious that
philosophers, and philosophers alone, are capable of
enjoying the good and happy life. If true happiness
is an excellence or "virtue" of the soul — a "rejoicing
of the soul" — then, too, happiness will be the exclusive possession of the philosophers or, at least, of the
majority of the philosophers. For virtue and a noble
character are the governing principles of our lives.
And by comparison, the intellectual life (*phronesis*)
is the most delightful of all things. We would reach a
similar conclusion if it were said that in their aggre-
gate all these things constitute true happiness. But,
whatever our definition (or conclusion), happiness
must always be defined in terms of intellectual endeavors (*phronein*).

— 92 —

Hence, all people who are capable of engaging in
philosophic speculation ought to do so. For philosophical speculation is either the ultimate good life or,
at least, most truly of all individual things the well-
spring for the good life of all souls.

— 93 —

At this point it might be appropriate to shed some additional light upon our subject [by quoting certain commonly held opinions about these matters].

— 94 —

To everyone, this much must by now be quite obvious: no one, not even a person who, like so many fools, delights in the pursuit of the most extravagant pleasures of the senses, would prefer to live a life of wealth and power and, at the same time, be wholly devoid of all intelligence and, as a matter of fact, be a complete moron. Thus it seems that all men avoid at all costs the loss of good sense. Now the opposite of senselessness or lack of good sense is intelligence (*phronesis*), and of two opposites one is always to be shunned and the other to be chosen.

— 95 —

Following up our discussion, we may state: as sickness is to be avoided, so is health to be desired. By the same token and in keeping with this argument, it appears that according to the commonly held opinion, philosophic knowledge (*phronesis*) is to be preferred above all other things, but certainly not because of anything that might result from it in a practical sense. For, even if a man were to possess everything in this world but were utterly corrupt and diseased of mind, his life would not be worth living, since even the other possessions or goods could not possibly profit him.

— 96 —

Hence, all men, if they ever come in contact with philosophic wisdom and get a chance to taste the works of the intellect, value all other things as nothing. And this is the reason why no one among us could endure being intoxicated or remaining a child forever.

— 97 —

For this same reason we must admit that sleep, although it is without doubt something pleasant, is not a thing to be preferred over waking, even though we might suppose that a person asleep experiences all possible pleasures. This is so because the images caused by sleep are unreal and false, while those of waking are real and true. Hence, sleep and waking differ only to the extent that the soul, when it is awake, often knows the truth, but when asleep, is always deceived. For the whole world of dreams is entirely false and unreal.

— 98 —

Moreover, the fact that most men shrink from death should indicate that the soul has a love for learning and knowing. For in doing so, the soul, which normally seeks what is apparent and knowable, shrinks from what it does not know, such as darkness and the unknown. This is, more than anything else, also the reason why we maintain that we ought to honor and revere, above anything else, those to whom we owe our greatest gifts [namely, to the gods]: those to whom we owe our ability to see the sun and the light, namely, our fathers and mothers. For they are, it appears, the ultimate occasion of our ability to think and to see. It is also for this same reason that we cherish and delight in things as well as in men that are near and dear to us, and call dear those whom we know. All this, then, demonstrates plainly that that which is knowable, apparent, and clear is something worthy of our love. And if that which is knowable and clear is worthy of our love, then knowledge and intellectual pursuits are likewise objects of our love.

— 99 —

Aside from all this, just as in the case of material goods where the same kind of possession is, as regards men, not conducive to both life and the good or happy life, so it is also with philosophic knowledge or wisdom (*phronesis*). For in my opinion we do not need the same kind of philosophic knowledge or wisdom as regards plain life that we need for living the perfect life. The majority of men may wholly be excused for doing this — for being satisfied with that sort of knowledge which is sufficient to lead a normal and plain life. These people, to be sure, wish for a higher form of happiness, but on the whole they are content if they can simply live. But unless one submits that we ought to endure life on any terms whatever, it would be simply ludicrous not to make every possible effort toward and pay the greatest attention to the acquisition of that sort of philosophic knowledge or wisdom (*phronesis*) by which the ultimate truth will be known.

— 100 —

This, one might know already from the following facts, provided one contemplates human life in the bright light [of reason]: in so doing one will discover that all the things men believe to be great are just "shadows on the wall." Hence, one may properly insist that man is really nothing, and that nothing human is sound and stable. Strength, size and beauty are simply a laugh and worth nothing. Beauty seems to be just beauty because we see nothing accurately and reliably.

— 101 —

If one were able to see as clearly as Lynceus is said to have seen — Lynceus saw through walls and trees — would one ever consider it endurable to look at a human being, especially seeing the miserable materials of which he is composed? Honors and reputation, things for which people are most emulated and envied, are but an indescribable humbug. To him who looks upon what is eternal and real, it seems quite idiotic to strive after such things. What, then, is there among human things or affairs that is great and long-lasting? Because of our inherent weakness as well as the shortness of our lives, I submit that even this [namely, honors and reputation] seems to be important.

— 102 —

Who among us, realizing these facts, would consider himself truly happy and blessed — who of us would do so, especially since all of us, as they say during the initiation rites, are from the very beginning constituted by nature as if destined for punishment? For the divinely inspired among the ancient sages tell us that the soul pays penalties and that we live (in this world) because we are punished (exiled?) for certain great sins we have committed.

— 103 —

And, indeed, the union of the soul with the body strikes us as being very much such a punishment. For, as the Etruscans are said often to torture prisoners of war by chaining human carcasses face to face with living men, matching part with part, so also the soul seems to be stretched throughout the body as well as tied to the sensitive parts of the body.

— 104 —

Men as wholes possess nothing of worth and have no reason to consider themselves perchance divine or blessed, except in so far as they possess reason and philosophic wisdom (*phronesis*). This alone of all our endowments seems to be deathless; this alone seems to be divine.

— 105 —

Since human life is capable of sharing in this faculty [of reasoning and of acquiring wisdom], however wretched and difficult it may be, it is yet so wisely ordained that man appears to be a god when compared with all other creatures.

— 106 —

For reason is "the divine dwelling in us" [either
Hermotimus or Anaxagoras said this], and because
of reason mortal life possesses a certain element or
aspect of the divine. This being so, we ought either
to pursue philosophy or bid farewell to life and depart from this world, because all other things seem
to be but utter nonsense and folly.

Brief Comments

(The numbers of the several comments correspond to the numbers of the respective fragments. For abbreviations, see Introduction: Collections of the Fragments, and Sources of Reconstruction.)

– 1 –

Stobaeus IV. 785; frag. 50 Rose; frag. 1 Walzer; frag. 1 Ross; frag. 1 Düring. — See also Isocrates, *Antidosis* 70; [Isocrates], *Ad Demonicum* 49. — Fragment 1, it goes without saying, was not a part of the original *Protrepticus*, but it may be used appropriately as an ideal "Introduction." — Themison, presumably a "king" on the Island of Cyprus, is difficult to identify. Around the year 350 B.C., there were nine important cities on Cyprus, each ruled by a "king." See Diodorus Siculus XVI. 42. 4. The *Protrepticus* was addressed (or dedicated) to this Themison with whom Aristotle might have been acquainted, possibly through a common friend, Eudemus, who himself was a Cypriot. (This would date the *Protrepticus* in the vicinity of Eudemus' death which occurred in 354 B.C.) Or else the connections between Aristotle and Themison may have been part of the common political and cultural interests that existed between Athenian colonists on Cyprus and some of the native princes. That such ties existed is brought out in Isocrates' three

Cyprian Discourses, namely, the *To Nicocles,* the *To Evagoras,* and the *Nicocles,* all of which were written after 371 B.C., the year Nicocles succeeded his father Evagoras to the throne of Cyprian Salamis. — The idea that wealthy people can afford to spend their money on education also appears in Plato, *Protagoras* 326C. Plato also complains that the education of the children of important and wealthy men is often sadly neglected. See, for instance, Plato, *Laches* 179A ff., and *ibid.* at 180B ff.; *Protagoras* 319E ff., and *ibid.* at 324C ff.; *Meno* 93A ff.; *Laws* 694D; *I Alcibiades* 118D ff.

— 2 —

Oxyrh. Papyr. IV. 666; Stobaeus III. 200; frag. 57 Rose; frag. 3 Walzer; frag. 3 Ross; frag. 2 Düring. — Stobaeus credits this passage to Aristotle, and many scholars ascribe it to the *Protrepticus.* As to its language and style, it may well be Aristotelian. In the form of an "Introduction" it seems to state the main topic and purpose of the *Protrepticus.* — See also Aristotle, *Eudemian Ethics* 1218 b 32 ff.: "All goods are either outside or in the soul, and of these, those in the soul are more desirable . . . For philosophic wisdom (prudence?), virtue, and pleasure are in the soul, and some or all of these appear to all people to be the end." Similar views are expressed by Plato, *Apology* 29DE: "You, my friend, . . . are you not ashamed of piling up the greatest amount of money and public honors and reputation, and, at the same time, caring so little about philosophic wisdom (*phronesis*) and truth and the greatest improvement of the soul, which you never consider or heed at all." Plato, *Euthydemus* 281AB: "And in the use of the goods . . . namely, earthly wealth and health and beauty, is not philosophic knowledge that which directs us to the right use of them. . . ? . . . Then in every possession and in every use of a thing (or good), is not philosophic knowledge that which gives a man not only good fortune but also true success? . . . For . . . what do possessions profit a man if he have neither good sense nor philosophic wisdom?" Plato, *Laws* 661AB: "For the goods of which the many speak [*scil.*, the worldly goods] are not really good . . . While to the just and pious all these things are the best of possessions, to the unjust they are all, including even health, the greatest of evils . . . [T]o live at all without justice and virtue, even though a man be rich in all the so-called goods of fortune, is the greatest of evils, if life be immoral. . . ." As a matter of fact, from the *Apology* to the *Laws*, Plato constantly preaches the distinction between "worldly goods" and "goods of the soul," and the subordinating of the former to the latter.

— 3 —

Oxyrh. Papyr. IV. 666; Stobaeus III. 200; frag. 57 Rose; frag. 3 Walzer; frag. 3 Ross; frag. 3 Düring. — Similar views are stated by Aristotle in *Politics* 1323 a 23 ff.: "Certainly no one will dispute the propriety of partitioning the goods into . . . external goods, goods of the body, and goods of the soul . . . [But] men differ about the degree or relative desirability of this or that good . . . To these people we reply by an appeal to facts which easily prove that men do not acquire or preserve virtue by the help of external goods, but external goods by the help of virtue; and that happiness . . . is most often found among those who possess the highest culture of the mind and character, and have only a moderate share of external goods . . ."

— 4 —

Oxyrh. Papyr. IV. 666; Stobaeus III. 200; frag. 57 Rose;

frag. 3 Walzer; frag. 3 Ross; frag. 4 Düring. — See also
Aristotle, *Nicomachean Ethics* 1094 b 16 ff.: "Earthly
goods . . . bring harm to many people . . . [M]en have
been undone by their wealth . . ." Aristotle, *Politics* 1323 b
8 ff.; *Rhetoric* 1355 b 6: "A man . . . can inflict the
greatest of injuries by the wrong use of [worldly] goods."
— The proverb, "surfeit begets insolence" or, "satiety
begets wantonness" is fairly common in Greek literature.

– 5 –

Oxyrh. Papyr. IV. 666; Stobaeus III. 200; frag. 57 Rose;
frag. 3 Walzer; frag. 3 Ross; frag. 5 Düring. — See also
Isocrates, *Antidosis* 285; Isocrates, *Ad Nicoclem* 35. —
Plato, in *Philebus* 58D, speaks of the soul as capable
of seeking the truth. In *Euthydemus* 282CD, Plato insists that "only wisdom can make a man happy and
fortunate," and that, therefore, "all of us ought to pursue
wisdom." And in *Euthydemus* 288D, he states: "Have
we not agreed that philosophy ought to be studied?"
— The "protreptic" (hortatory) nature of the Platonic
Euthydemus has long been recognized.

– 6 –

Alex. of Aphrod., *Top.*, CIAG II. 2. 149,9; frag. 51 Rose;
frag. 2 Walzer; frag. 2 Ross; frag. 6 Düring. — See here
also Cicero, *Tuscul. Disput.* III. 3. 6 (Cicero, *Hortensius*,
frag. 4 Müller); Quintilian, *Institutio Oratoria* V. 10. 70;
Clement of Alexandria, *Stromateis* VI. 18 (p. 168,
Stählin) Lactantius, *Institutiones Divinae* III. 16. 9 (Cicero, *Hortensius*, frag. 12 Müller); Boethius, *De Differentiis
Topicis* 2. Tradition has it that in the *Protrepticus* Aristotle had stated something like this: "You say that one
should (or must) philosophize; then you should (or
must) philosophize. You say that one should not (or

must not) philosophize, then (in order to prove your con-
tention) you must philosophize. In any event, you must
philosophize." (There are several variations of this statement.) In this particular form the above statement, *pace*
all historians of formal logic, cannot be found in the
Aristotelian *Protrepticus*. The history of this statement is
probably the following: Alexander of Aphrodisias (*Top.*,
CIAG II. 2. p. 149,9 ff.) merely reports that according
to Aristotle's *Protrepticus* "the expression 'to philosophize' implies two distinct things: first, whether or not
we ought at all seek [after philosophic truth] . . ." This
bit of extremely meager information does not entitle us to
assume that Aristotle's *Protrepticus* actually contained
the above-mentioned involved "logical argument." Some
Neo-Platonic commentators (Olympiodorus, *Commentarius in Platonis Alcibiadem*, edit. F. Creuzer, p. 144;
Elias, *Commentaria in Porphyrii Isagogen et in Aristotelis
Categorias*, CIAG XVIII. 1. p. 3,17-23; David, *Prolegomena et in Porphyrii Isagogen Commentarium*, CIAG
XVIII. 2. p. 9,2-12; and Anonymous, *Scholia in Aristotelis
Analytica Priora*, Cod. Paris. 2064, fol. 263a), it appears,
by relying on the cryptic statement of Alexander of
Aphrodisias, as well as some other ancient authors, made
liberal and obviously unwarranted additions and altera-
tions of their own. — It is difficult to ascertain accurately
just what Aristotle means by the terms "to philosophize"
and "philosophy." In *Republic* 475C, Plato points out
that "he who has a taste of every kind of knowledge and
who is eager and curious to learn and is never satisfied,
may properly be called a philosopher." See also Plato,
Theaetetus 175E. For additional Platonic definitions of
philosophy, see, for instance, Plato, *Republic* 468E, and
ibid. at 475B; 475E; 480A; 484D; 485AB; 502C; 525B;
537CD; 582DE; *et passim; Sophist* 249CD, and *ibid.* at
254A; *Phaedo* 65E; *Symposium* 218A; etc.

— 7 —

Iamblich., *Protrep.* 36,27-37,3; frag. 7 Düring. — Fragment 7, like fragments 8 and 9, contains only brief and somewhat garbled excerpts or condensations which might, or might not, originally have been taken from the *Protrepticus*. Plato, in *Laws* 732E, likewise states: "For it is to men that we are speaking, and not to gods." — See also Aristotle, *Eudemian Ethics* 1215 a 35 ff.: ". . . there are three lives which all those choose who have power, namely, the life of the politician, of the philosopher, and of the voluptuary . . ."

— 8 —

Iamblich., *Protrep.* 37,3-11; frag. 4 Walzer; frag. 4 Ross; frag. 8 Düring. — See also fragment 7, *supra*, and the comments thereto; Cicero, *Hortensius* frag. 23 Müller. — This particular fragment contains five propositions: (1) the body is a tool; (2) the use of any tool is always risky; (3) the improper use of the body (or, of a tool) is harmful; (4) we must learn how to use tools properly; and (5) if we wish to be good rulers we ought to become philosophers. This sounds somewhat like Plato, *Euthydemus* 280D-282D: (1) good things must not only be possessed, but also used properly; (2) evil will result from the wrong use of good things; (3) knowledge of the proper use of things is required; (4) without rational knowledge and philosophic wisdom all our possessions are worthless; and (5) this being so we ought to become philosophers and philosophize. It is by no means impossible, and as a matter of fact quite probable, that in this instance the *Protrepticus* is under the influence of Plato's *Euthydemus* which, it has been pointed out, contains hortatory elements. Some scholars believe that Iamblichus actually quotes here from the Platonic

Euthydemus (and, perhaps, from Plato's *First Alcibiades* 129C-135A, and from the *Statesman* 289D-290E; 303D-305C) rather than from the *Protrepticus.*

— 9 —

Iamblich., *Protrep.* 31,11-22; frag. 4 Walzer; frag. 4 Ross; frag. 9 Düring. — See also fragment 7, *supra,* and the corresponding comments; Cicero, *Hortensius* frag. 68 Müller. — There exists a certain affinity between frag. 9 and Plato's *Euthydemus* and *Statesman* (see comments to fragment 8, *supra*), as well as Aristotle's *Physics* 194 b 1 ff., and *Metaphysics* 982 a 17 ff. — Aristotle might possibly have borrowed the notion of the "correctness of judgment" from Plato. See, for instance, Plato, *Meno* 97B ff., *Laws* 689B, and *ibid.* at 689D. But in his later works, Aristotle insists that this "correctness of judgment" is a "gift of nature." See, for instance, Aristotle, *Topics* 116 b 10; *Nicomachean Ethics* 1143 b 6; *Rhetoric* 1365 a 29.

— 10 —

Iamblich., *Protrep.* 49,3-11; frag. 11 Walzer; frag. 11 Ross; frag. 11 Düring. — Similar views are expressed by Aristotle in *Physics* 196 b 22 ff.: "Events that are for the sake of something include whatever may be done as a result of thought or nature." *Ibid.* at 197 a 2 ff.: "[A certain conduct] belongs to the class of things that are intentional and the result of intelligent deliberation." See also Plato, *Laws* 889A: "They say that the greatest and fairest things are the work of nature as well as that of chance, the lesser that of art which, receiving from nature the greater and original creations, moulds and fashions all those lesser works which are generally called 'artificial.'" *Ibid.* at 709B: "God governs all things, and

chance and art co-operate with Him in the government
of human affairs." — The tripartition, nature-art-chance,
which can also be found in Pre-Socratic philosophy, is
mentioned in Aristotle, *Posterior Analytics* 95 a 7; *Physics*
198 a 9-10; *Metaphysics* 1032 a 12, and *ibid.* at 1070
a 6; *Eudemian Ethics* 1223 a 10-12; *Nicomachean Ethics*
1140 a 10-16; *Rhetoric* 1368 b 36-37. It was severely
criticized by Plato in *Laws* 889B ff.

— 11 —

Iamblich., *Protrep.* 49,11-25; frag. 11 Walzer; frag. 11
Ross; frag. 12 Düring. — The ideas advanced here apparently were elaborated in greater detail in Aristotle,
Physics 196 b 10 ff.: "First, then, we observe that
some things come into being in the same way always,
and others do so usually. It is clearly of neither of these
that chance is said to be the cause . . . But there is a
third class of events . . . events which everyone says
are 'by chance' . . . Secondly, some events are for the
sake of something, others not. Again, some of the former
class are in accordance with deliberate intent, others not.
But both are in the class of things which are for the
sake of something. Hence it is clear that even among the
things which are outside the necessary and normal, there
are some in relation to which the expression, 'for the
sake of something,' is applicable . . . Things of this kind,
then, when they come into being accidentally, are said
to be 'by chance.' . . . That which is *per se* cause of
the effect is determinate, but the incidental cause is in-
determinable. For the possible attributes of an individual are innumerable . . ."

— 12 —

Iamblich., *Protrep.* 49,26-50,12; frag. 11 Walzer; frag.

11 Ross; frag. 13 Düring. — The view that art imitates
nature had already been expressed by Democritus. See
comments to fragment 10, *supra.*— In *Physics* 199 b 8
ff., Aristotle discusses in detail the notion that things
have a purpose, and that some things achieve their perfection (or purpose) by themselves, while others need
"assistance." In *Politics* 1337 a 1 ff., Aristotle maintains
that art and education seek to make up for the deficiencies of nature.

— 13 —

Iamblich., *Protrep.* 50,12-19; frag. 11 Walzer; frag. 11
Ross; frag. 14 Düring. — The notions that everything
comes into being properly, comes into being for a purpose,
that whatever turns out to be good and beautiful comes
into being properly, and that everything coming into
being according to nature, turns out to be good and
beautiful, are Platonic (and Aristotelian). See also Plato,
Charmides 165D: "If you were to ask me, what is the
result or effect of architecture . . . I would say houses,
and likewise of other arts which all have their different
results." Aristotle, in *Magna Moralia* 1190 a 11 ff., states:
"Does it belong to the science of house-building to de-
sign the end rightly . . . ?" — Some scholars insist that although the *Magna Moralia* in its present form definitely
betrays post-Aristotelian influences and post-Aristotelian
"editorial work," its first version may very well date
back to the earliest period of Aristotle's literary activities.

— 14 —

Iamblich., *Protrep.* 50,19-26; frag. 11 Walzer; frag. 11
Ross; frag. 15 Düring. — See here also Xenophon, *Memorabilia* I. 4. 6. — There exist rather striking similarities
between this fragment and certain passages in Aristotle's

De Partibus Animalium, passim, especially at 639 b 19
ff., and ibid. at 645 a 25.

— 15 —

Iamblich., Protrep. 50,27-51,6; frag. 11 Walzer; frag. 11
Ross; frag. 16 Düring. — See also Xenophon, Memorabilia
I. 4. 14. — In Physics 193 a 1, Aristotle distinguishes
between "by nature" and "according to nature," the
latter signifying something that fully coincides with "nature's plan." Disease, for instance, is "by nature," but
certainly not "according to nature." — In Physics 194 a
34, Aristotle maintains that "we use everything as if it
were there for our own sake." Politics 1253 a 31: "Man,
when perfected, is the best of animals."

— 16 —

Iamblich., Protrep. 51,7-10; frag. 11 Walzer; frag. 11
Ross; frag. 18 Düring. — For the "quotation" from Pythagoras, see also Iamblichus, Vita Pythagorae 12,58-59;
Cicero, Tuscul. Disput. V. 3. 8; and comments to fragment 42, infra. — The identification of "nature" and "God"
can be found in Aristotle, De Caelo 271 a 33: "God
and nature create nothing that is without use." It has
been said that Aristotle's teleological approach implies
the "presence" of a principle which, akin to a kind of
"divine providence," guides everything to its proper end.
See also Aristotle, Nicomachean Ethics 1179 b 21-22:
"Nature's part . . . [is] but the result of some divine
causes . . ." It may be presumed that for Aristotle "God"
signifies, in this instance, something like "the order in
nature," primarily.

— 17 —

Iamblich., *Protrep.* 51,11-15; frag. 11 Walzer; frag. 11
Ross; frag. 19 Düring. — See Clement of Alexandria,
Stromateis II. 130. — According to Diogenes Laertius
II. 7, Anaxagoras declared the heavens to be his true
fatherland. See also *ibid.* at II. 10: "When asked to what
end he [*scil.*, Anaxagoras] was born, he replied, 'to study
the sun and the moon and the heavens.'" See also
Eudemian Ethics 1216 a 1 ff.: ". . . Anaxagoras answered
a man. . . asking why one should choose rather to be
born than not: 'For the sake of viewing the heavens
and the whole order of the universe.'"

— 18 —

Iamblich., *Protrep.* 51,16-52,5; frag. 11 Walzer; frag. 11
Ross; frag. 17 Düring. — The notion that man comes into
being for the purpose of "reasoning," or for using his
reason, on the whole is Platonic (and Aristotelian). The
statement that the excellence of old age rests on "the
wisdom of age," which is man's last acquisition, is Platonic.
Aside from Plato's insistence that only "elderly people"
should become guardians in the perfect city (see *Republic, passim; Laws, passim*), he suggests, in *Theaetetus* 186BC, that nature endows men as well as animals with simple sensations at birth, but philosophic wisdom and speculation are slowly and painfully acquired
through education and long experience. See Aristotle,
Nicomachean Ethics 1142 a 15: ". . . a young man has
no experience, for it is the length of time that gives experience." In *Politics* 1334 b 14: "In man rational principle and the intellect are the ends towards which nature strives." *Ibid.* at 1334 b 22: ". . . anger and desire
and wanting are implanted in children from their very

birth, but reason and understanding are developed as
they grow older."

— 19 —

Iamblich., *Protrep.* 52,6-11; frag. 11 Walzer; frag. 11
Ross; frag. 20 Düring. — The statement ascribed to Pythagoras, that "every man was created by God for the purpose of acquiring knowledge and engaging in contemplation," cannot be identified. It may or may not be by
Pythagoras. It might possibly be connected with Pythagoras' alleged definition of a "philosopher." See comments to fragment 42, *infra.* — Plato, in *Timaeus* 47A
ff., insists that "God devised and gave us sight to the
end that we might behold the courses of the intelligences
in the heavens . . ." See also Aristotle, *De Caelo* 271
a 33: "But God and nature create nothing that is without
some use." *De Generatione et Corruptione* 336 b 31:
"God, therefore, adopted the remaining alternative and
completed the perfection of the universe. . ." *Nicomachean Ethics* 1153 b 32: "For all things have by nature something divine in them." *Ibid.* at 1179 b 21 ff.:
"Nature's part evidently does not depend on us, but as
the result of some divine causes is present in those who
are truly fortunate . . ." — The term *phronesis,* as used
here and elsewhere in the *Protrepticus,* may mean any
of the following: practical wisdom, speculative wisdom,
intuitive wisdom, skilled "know-how," rational knowledge,
reasoning, etc.

— 20 —

Iamblich., *Protrep.* 52,12-16; frag. 11 Walzer; frag. 11
Ross; frag. 21 Düring. — Similar notions are expressed
by Plato in *Euthydemus* 279A ff. — Here Aristotle crypti-

cally states, perhaps for the first time, what he announces
later (?) in *Metaphysics* (book A) 982 b 4-6: there is a
"science" that knows to what end each thing must be
done; and this particular science is the most authoritative of all the sciences. Both the *Protrepticus* (Iamblich.,
Protrep. 52,12-16) and *Metaphysics*, book A, proclaim
what seems to be a bit of Platonism, namely, that wisdom concerned with practical issues is the highest form
of wisdom or "the first wisdom" ("metaphysics"). In his
later metaphysical treatises, "metaphysics" or "the first
wisdom" is concerned with being *qua* being. This might
lend some support to the claim that book A of the *Metaphysics* is a very early work of Aristotle and as such
is "Platonic" or, at least, partly "Platonic."

— 21 —

Iamblich., *Protrep.* 34,5-16; frag. 23 Düring. — Like fragments 22-28, *infra*, this particular fragment may or may
not be part of the original *Protrepticus*. If fragments
21-28 are actually citations from Aristotle, they are in all
likelihood seriously abridged and severely mutilated. As
a result they strike us as being disjointed. — The idea
that nature does nothing at random can be found throughout the works of Aristotle. The notion that art imitates
nature (in Plato it imitates "an imitation of the true es-
sences") can be found, for instance, in Aristotle, *Mete-
orologica* 381 b 6, and *ibid.* at 396 b 11; that the soul is
better than the body, in *De Generatione Animalium*
731 b 29; that the body exists for the sake of the soul,
in *Eudemian Ethics* 1241 b 23 ff.; and that the soul has
a rational as well as an irrational part, in *Nicomachean
Ethics* 1098 a 2, and *ibid.* at 1102 a 28; 1102 b 13;
1102 b 29; 1119 b 15; 1138 b 8; 1139 a 5; 1168 b 21;
1172 b 10; 1182 a 24 ff.; *Magna Moralia* 1185 b 1 ff.,
and *ibid.* at 1196 b 14; *Eudemian Ethics* 1219 b 26; etc.

— It is fair to assume that the Aristotelian bipartition of the soul suggested here is under the influence of Plato's well-known doctrine of the tripartite soul. See, for instance, Plato, *Republic* 435B ff., and *ibid.* at 504A; 550A; 580E ff.; *Timaeus* 69E ff., and *ibid.* at 89E; *Laws* 896D; etc.

— 22 —

Iamblich., *Protrep.* 34,17-22; frag. 24 Düring. — Aristotle maintains here that the function of reason is (speculative) thinking, and that (speculative) thinking is "visual perception of the intelligible things." He also expresses similar views in *De Anima* 426 a 13.

— 23 —

Iamblich., *Protrep.* 34,22-26; frag. 25 Düring. — The notion that "intellectual activities pursued for their own sake are superior to intellectual activities pursued for the sake of something else" has been restated by Aristotle several times: *Metaphysics* 982 b 4; and *ibid.* at 1075 a 19-23; *Politics* 1325 b 17-23. The idea that only those intellectual activities are truly "free" which are pursued for their own sake reappears in *Metaphysics* 982 b 27, where the "most authoritative science," the "first philosophy," is called "the only free science, because it alone exists for its own sake." In *Theaetetus* 173BC, Plato insists that the brotherhood of philosophers is "a brotherhood that is free." See also *ibid.* at 175E: ". . . the free man . . . whom we call philosopher."

— 24 —

Iamblich., *Protrep.* 34,27-35,5; frag. 26 Düring. — Here Aristotle reduces the soul-body relation to a master-servant relation. Also, reliance on the body means reliance on chance, while reliance on the soul always bodes well. See also *Magna Moralia* 1207 a 4-5: "Hence, wherever there is the greatest intellect and reason, there is least chance; and wherever there is most chance, there is least mind." *Ibid.* at 1207 a 18-20: "Good fortune and fortune (chance) generally manifest themselves in things that are not within our power, and of which we are neither the master nor are able to effect them."

— 25 —

Iamblich., *Protrep.* 35,6-14; frag. 27 Düring. — Here Aristotle not only distinguishes between practical wisdom and intuitive (or speculative) knowledge, but he also affirms the superiority of the latter — definitely a Platonic twist.

— 26 —

Iamblich., *Protrep.* 35,14-18; frag. 28 Düring. — Note the Aristotelian "scale": a man without senses and without reason is a plant; a man without reason is a brute beast; a man fully possessing reason and acting according to the dictates of his reason is god-like. This is Aristotle's classification of animate life in (1) "the ability to take food," (2) "the ability to have sense perceptions," and (3) "the ability to reason." The notion that man without reason is a brute beast can be found also in Plato, *Charmides* 155DE; *Phaedrus* 233A; *Republic* 571C; and *Timaeus* 70E. The idea that the proper use of reason (or the proper practice of philosophy) makes man god-like — the *homoiosis* doctrine — is definitely Platonic (or Pythagorean?). See, for instance, Plato, *Theaetetus* 176B; *Republic* 500CD; and *Sophist* 216BC.

– 27 –

Iamblich., *Protrep.* 36,7-13; frag. 29 Düring. – In *Meta-physics* 982 b 27 ff., Aristotle intimates that "knowledge for knowledge's sake" (or, purely theoretical or specu-lative wisdom) "might very well be beyond human pow-er." This notion, which also is expressed in fragment 29, though properly modified by Iamblichus, seems to be Platonic, as might be seen, for instance, in Plato, *Phaedrus* 278D: "Wise . . . is a great name that belongs to God alone." In *De Anima* 421 a 30, Aristotle points out that man's sensory perceptions as a rule are inferior to those of animals. See also Aristotle, *Historia Animalium* 494 b 18; *De Generatione Animalium* 781 b 17.

– 28 –

Iamblich., *Protrep.* 36,13-20; frag. 30 Düring. – The no-tion expressed here by Iamblichus seems to restate in a greatly compressed form Plato, *Gorgias* 526DE: "Re-nouncing the honors after which the world strives, I desire only to know the truth, and to live as well as I can; and when I die, to die as well as I can. And, to the utmost of my powers, I exhort all other men to do the same. . . And I exhort you also to take part in that great combat, which is the conflict of life, and is greater than any other earthly conflict."

– 29 –

Iamblich., *Protrep.* 37,22-26; frag. 52 Rose; frag. 5 Wal-zer; frag. 5 Ross; frag. 31 Düring. – Plato, *Republic* 496CD, likewise points out the difficulties connected with living the life of a philosopher, difficulties which are often incommensurate with the practical usefulness of philosophy itself. – Anaximenes of Lampsacus, in his

Ars Rhetorica (p. 14,26-15,1, edit. Spengel-Hammer), and Aristotle, to some extent, in his *Rhetorica ad Alexandrum* 1421 b 23-27, point out that first of all we must determine what is just, what is expedient, what is useful, what is proper, what is desirable, what is easily achieved, what is possible, and what is necessary.

— 30 —

Iamblich., *Protrep.* 37,26-38,3; frag. 52 Rose; frag. 5 Walzer; frag. 5 Ross; frag. 32 Düring. — This badly mutilated fragment contains a subdivision of philosophy (or, of scientific knowledge) into what we would call "ethics" and "metaphysics" (or "physics"). But the interdependence of these two subdivisions is not discussed. In Iamblich., *Math. Scient.* 79,10-15, similar views are advanced, though in a different version and probably in a somewhat more garbled fashion. See here also Plato, *Philebus* 58E-59A.

— 31 —

Iamblich., *Protrep.* 38,3-14 (see also Iamblich., *Math. Scient.* 81,7-16); frag. 52 Rose; frag. 5 Walzer; frag. 5 Ross; frag. 33 Düring. — The Platonic doctrine of Ideas always implies that the Idea (the "better") is more knowable than the corporeal thing (the "lesser" — *Republic* 505A, and *ibid.* at 532A ff.); that the Idea (the "prior") is more knowable than the corporeal thing (the "posterior" — *Republic* 475E ff., *Symposium* 211BC); that the "determinate" and the "ordered" (the Ideas) are more knowable than the "indeterminate" and the "disordered" (corporeal things — *Republic* 479E, and *ibid.* at 500BC; 587A; 619CD; *Philebus* 59C ff.; *Phaedrus* 256AB; *Phaedo* 79A; *Statesman* 305CD; *Timaeus* 47DE; *Laws* 780E); that the better is more "determinate" and more "ordered" than the "lesser" (*Gorgias* 504A ff.; *Philebus* 64D ff., and *ibid.* at 66A; *Timaeus* 30A); that the Ideas as the "causes" of corporeal things are more knowable than the corporeal things (their "effects" — *Republic* 508E ff., and *ibid.* at 509D); that the "prior" is more "cause" than the "posterior" (*ibid.*); and that if we were to do away with the Ideas we would utterly destroy the power of reasoning and, hence, make true knowledge impossible (*Parmenides* 135B ff.) — In *Topics* 141 b 5 ff., and *Metaphysics* 1019 a 1 ff., Aristotle points out that the prior is more knowable than the posterior; in *De Partibus Animalium* 641 b 18 ff., he insists that "order and definiteness are much more plainly manifest in the [perfect] celestial bodies than in our own frame"; in *Metaphysics* 982 a 14 ff., he announces that "he who is more exact and more capable of teaching the causes is the wiser man"; and *ibid.* at 1017 b 17 ff., he maintains that if "the parts which are present in such things, limiting (defining) and making them as individual things," are destroyed, the whole is destroyed due to the destruction of the parts, "as the solid is destroyed by the destruction of the plane . . . and the plane by the destruction of the line." — The sequence of solid, plane, and line can also be found in Plato. See, for instance, *Meno* 82B ff.; *Republic* 509E ff., and *ibid.* at 528AB; *Theaetetus* 148AB; *Statesman* 299E; *Philebus* 51C; *Timaeus* 55E.

— 32 —

Iamblich., *Protrep.* 38,14-22; frag. 52 Rose; frag. 5 Walzer; frag. 5 Ross; frag. 34 Düring. — Plato, in *Gorgias* 464A ff., points out that "there are many persons who appear to be in good physical health, and whom only a physician or trainer can diagnose at first sight not to be in good health . . . The soul and the body . . .

have two arts corresponding to them . . .[T]he art concerned with the body . . . has two subdivisions, one
of them being gymnastics, the other medicine . . ." See
also *ibid.* at 517E-518A: ". . . [the] art of gymnastics
and [the art of] medicine . . . are the true ministers
of the physical body . . ." Plato, *Sophist* 228E-229A:
"And in the case of the body, are there not two arts
which are dealing with the [body]. . .? There is gymnastics . . . and medicine . . ." — In the *De Partibus Animalium* 644 b 25 ff., Aristotle likewise insists that "things
. . . ungenerated, imperishable, and eternal . . . are
excellent beyond comparison . . . but less accessible to
knowledge. The evidence [of them] . . . is furnished
but sparingly by the senses."

— 33 —

Iamblich., *Protrep.* 38, 22-39,4 (see also Iamblich., *Math.
Scient.* 81,20-24); frag. 52 Rose; frag. 5 Walzer; frag.
5 Ross; frag. 35 Düring. — The ideas expressed here are
elaborated, for instance, in Aristotle, *Metaphysics* 1003
a 21-32; *Topics* 141 b 6 ff., where we are told that
the "prior" is more intelligible than the "posterior"; and in
Metaphysics 982 a 13, where we are informed that he
who knows causes is always the wiser. See also *ibid.*
at 982 b 28 ff., and 1003 b 16 ff.; and comments to
fragment 31, *supra.*

— 34 —

Iamblich., *Protrep.* 39,4-8; frag. 52 Rose; frag. 5 Walzer;
frag. 5 Ross; frag. 36 Düring. — Aristotle refers here to
the first "principle" or "stuff" advocated by Heraclitus of
Ephesus ("fire"), Anaxagoras ("air"), or Pythagoras
("number"). In *Physics* 184 a 10, Aristotle states that
only through the knowledge of first principles can we

attain scientific knowledge. See also *ibid.* at 194 b 19;
Metaphysics 983 a 25, and *ibid.* at 993 b 23; 994 b
29; 1003 a 26; 1025 b 6. — The notion that one had to
know syllables first in order to recognize articulate speech,
and letters in order to recognize syllables, can also be
found in Plato, *Statesman* 277E ff., and *ibid.* at 285CD;
Theaetetus 201E; *Cratylus* 424E; *Timaeus* 48BC. But already Democritus had used the analogy between atoms
composing things and letters making up words. See fragment 31, *supra.*

— 35 —

Iamblich., *Protrep.* 39,9-11; frag. 52 Rose; frag. 5 Walzer;
frag. 5 Ross; frag. 37 Düring. — See here also Iamblich.,
Math. Scient. 81,5-7.

— 36 —

Iamblich., *Protrep.* 39,11-16; frag. 52 Rose; frag. 5 Walzer; frag. 5 Ross; frag. 38 Düring. — The passage, "law
alone is the ruler and it alone has authority," may be
Aristotle's version of Pindar's statement: "Law is the king
of all, mortals as well as immortals, ruling with absolute authority (or, with the greatest of highhandedness)."
Frag. 169 Bergk; frag. 151 Böckh. Plato, in *Gorgias* 484B,
"misquotes" (intentionally?) Pindar when he says: "Law
is the king of all, mortals and immortals, makes might
to be right, doing violence in the most highhanded manner . . ." In *Protagoras* 337D, Plato maintains that "law
is the tyrant of mankind, often compelling us to do things
which are against our nature." See also Plato, *Laws*
690BC, and *ibid.* at 714A ff.; 715A. The notion that
true law is the expression of philosophic wisdom or of
the "right philosophy," also appears in Plato, *Statesman*
293CD.

— 37 —

Iamblich., *Protrep.* 39,16-20; frag. 52 Rose; frag. 5 Walzer; frag. 5 Ross; frag. 39 Düring. — Aristotle's remark
that the "wise man" (the true philosopher) is the most
accurate standard (or norm) of what is right, might be
under the influence of Plato, *Republic, passim, Statesman,
passim,* and especially *Theaetetus* 178B ff. *Ibid.* at
178B, Plato takes up Protagoras' criterion, to wit, that
"man is the measure of all things." *Ibid.* at 179B, Plato
argues that "the wise man is the measure." And *ibid.* at
183C, he insists that "only the wise man is the measure."
In *Laws* 875C, Plato insists that "if a man were born so
divinely gifted that he could naturally apprehend the
truth, he would not stand in need of laws to rule over
him. For there is no law . . . which is above knowledge,
nor can the intellect . . . be deemed the subject or
slave of any man, but rather the lord of all." Plato,
Statesman 293A ff., and *ibid.* at 297E ff. See here also
Aristotle, *Nicomachean Ethics* 1113 a 32 ff.: ". . . the
good man . . . sees the truth in each class of things,
being as it were the measure and norm of them." *Ibid.*
at 1128 a 31 ff.: "The refined and well-bred man . . .
[is] as it were a norm or standard unto himself." *Ibid.*
at 1176 a 17 ff.: ". . . virtue and the good man as such
are the measure of each thing." See, furthermore, *ibid.*
at 1105 b 5 ff.; 1107 a 1; 1166 a 10 ff.; 1176 b 25;
Eudemian Ethics 1249 a 21 ff.

— 38 —

Iamblich., *Protrep.* 39,20-40, 1 (see also Iamblich., *Math.
Scient.* 82,4-11); frag. 52 Rose; frag. 5 Walzer; frag. 5
Ross; frag. 40 Düring. — Here Aristotle refers to Plato's
well-known four cardinal virtues: justice, fortitude, temperance, and wisdom. The just man lives justly, that is,

"he does his work" in keeping with the Platonic notion
that it is the end of everything "to do its proper work,"
to wit, the end of the just man is to do justice, etc.
See also Aristotle, *Nicomachean Ethics* 1176 a 26 ff.,
where we are told that the good man always does what
is in accordance with virtue, and that which is in accordance with virtue is always the most valuable and pleasant thing.

— 39 —

Iamblich., *Protrep.* 41,6-15; frag. 6 Walzer; frag. 6 Ross;
frag. 41 Düring. — See here also Iamblich., *Math. Scient.*
80, 1-81,4. — The ideas expressed, namely, that intellectual
activity (and wisdom) is desirable on its own account and,
at the same time, useful for practical life, has been restated many times by Plato and Aristotle. For only philosophy or philosophic wisdom enables us to ascertain what
is the truly good life (or virtue or wisdom). See, for
instance, Plato, *Republic* 581E, and *ibid.* at 586A ff.;
Laws 697B, and *ibid.* at 743E; etc.; Aristotle, *Magna
Moralia* 1184 b 1 ff.; *Politics* 1323 a 24 ff.; *Nicomachean
Ethics* 1174 a 20 ff., and *ibid.* at 1177 a 19 ff.; etc.

— 40 —

Iamblich., *Protrep.* 52,16-53,2 (see also Iamblich., *Math.
Scient.* 82, 11-13); frag. 58 Rose; frag. 12 Walzer; frag.
12 Ross; frag. 42 Düring. — In *Lysis* 220A ff., Plato maintains that the things which are loved for the sake of something else are only *called* dear. Only that for the sake
of which these things are loved *is* really dear to us. In
Republic 558D ff., Plato distinguishes between "necessary" and "unnecessary" pleasures. Necessary pleasures
are those of which "we cannot rid ourselves, and of
which the satisfaction is beneficial to us. . . . [B]ecause we

are constituted by nature so as to desire both what is
beneficial and what is necessary . . . And the desires
of which a man divests himself, if he takes pains from
his youth on — of which the presence, however, does no
good and in some instances the reverse of good — . . .
all these pleasures are unnecessary . . ." See also *ibid.*
at 493A ff.; 525B ff.; *Statesman* 281DE. Similar views can
be found in Aristotle, *Nicomachean Ethics* 1147 a 23
ff., and *ibid.* at 1096 b 16 ff.: "What sort of goods would
one call 'good' in themselves? Is it those which are pursued even when isolated from others [*scil.,* from other
goods], such as intelligence, sight, and certain pleasures
and honors? Certainly, provided we pursue these also
for the sake of something else. Nevertheless, one would
reckon them also among things good in themselves."
Politics 1338 b 2 ff.: "To be always seeking after the
useful is not becoming free and exalted souls." — The
notion that there cannot be an "infinite series" is also
found in *Physics* 256 a 3 ff., and *ibid.* at 241 a 24 ff.;
Metaphysics 994 b 9 ff.; *Posterior Analytics* 83 b 28;
Nicomachean Ethics 1094 a 19 ff. — The obviously polem-
ic character of the first part of fragment 40 would
suggest that it is part of a determined refutation of
Isocrates and his school of rhetoric. In *Antidosis* 258-269,
Isocrates had stated: "[E]ven among the professors of
disputation [Isocrates might here refer to the Academy
and, perhaps, to Aristotle who, as it is known, gave
instruction in rhetoric at the Academy long before the
year 353 B.C., *note by the present author*] there are
some who talk . . . abusively of the art of speaking on
general and useful topics . . . because they think that
by denouncing this art they will enhance their own
standing. I could, perhaps, say much nastier things of
them than they are saying of me, but I shall refrain
from doing so for two reasons. I wish neither to descend
to the level of men whom envy has made blind, nor to

censure men who, although they do no actual harm to
their pupils, are less able to benefit them than are other
teachers. However, I shall say a few words about them,
first, because they have paid their compliments to me;
secondly, in order that you, being better informed as
to their powers, may estimate us fairly in relation to
each other; and, finally, that I may show you clearly
that we, who are occupied with political discourse and
whom they call contentious, are more considerate than
they are. For although they are always saying disparag-
ing things about me, I shall not answer them in kind,
but shall confine myself to the simple truth. For I believe that the teachers who are skilled in eristic disputation and those who are preoccupied with astronomy and
geometry and studies of this sort do not injure but, on
the contrary, benefit their pupils, not so much as they
claim, but certainly more than others give them credit
for. Most men see in such studies nothing but empty
talk and hair-splitting; for none of these disciplines has
any useful [practical] application either to private or to
public affairs; nay, they are not even remembered for
any length of time after they are learned because they
do not attend us through life nor do they assist us in
what we do, but are wholly divorced from our practical
necessities. I am not of this opinion; on the other hand,
I am not far removed from it. Rather it seems to me
that those who consider this training to be of no use in
practical life and those who speak in praise of it, both
have truth on their side. If there is a contradiction in
this statement, it is because these disciplines are different in nature from the other studies which make
up our education. For the other branches are of use
to us only after we have gained a knowledge of them,
whereas these studies can be of no benefit to us after
we have mastered them unless we have elected to
make our living from this source, and they help us only

while we are in the process of learning. For while we
are occupied with the subtlety and exactness of astronomy and geometry and are forced to apply our minds
to difficult problems, and, in addition, are in the habit
of speaking and applying ourselves to what is said and
shown to us, not of letting our wits go wool-gathering,
we gain the power, after being exercised and sharpened
on these disciplines, of grasping and learning more
easily and more quickly those subjects which are of more
importance and of greater value. I do not, however,
think it proper to apply the term 'philosophy' to a training which is of no help to us in the present either in our
speech or in our actions, but rather I would call it a
gymnastics of the mind and a preparation for philosophy.
It is, to be sure, a study more advanced than that which
boys in school pursue, but it is for the most part the same
sort of thing. For after they have labored through their
lessons in grammar, music, and the other branches [of
liberal studies], they are not a whit advanced in their
ability to speak and deliberate on practical affairs, but
they have increased their aptitude for mastering greater
and more serious studies. I would, therefore, advise
young men to spend some time in these disciplines, but
not to allow their minds to be dried up by these barren
subtleties, nor to be stranded on the speculations of the
ancient sophists [*scil.*, philosophers] . . . For I think that
such curiosities of thought are on a par with the juggler's
tricks which, though they profit no one, still nonetheless
attract great crowds of empty-headed people, and I
hold that men who want to do some good in this world
must banish utterly from their interests all vain speculations and all activities which have no [practical] bearing
on our lives." — It should be noticed that Callicles, in
Plato's *Gorgias* 484CD, voices similar views about the
study of speculative philosophy. — An attack on the
Antidosis may also be seen in Aristotle, *Nicomachean*

Ethics, book 10, chap. 10.

— 41 —

Iamblich., *Protrep.* 53,2-15; frag. 58 Rose; frag. 12 Walzer; frag. 12 Ross; frag. 43 Düring. — See also Cicero, *De Finibus* V. 19. 53; Cicero, *Hortensius* frag. 50 Müller (St. Augustine, *De Trinitate* XIV. 9. 12). — Plato refers to the Islands of the Blessed in *Gorgias* 523B, and *ibid.* at 526C; *Menexenus* 235C; *Republic* 519C; and *Symposium* 180B. See also Aristotle, *Politics* 1334 a 28 ff.: ". . . those . . . who dwell in the Islands of the Blessed, they above all will need philosophy . . ." Descriptions of Hades as a place of punishment are found in Plato, *Phaedo* 108AB, and *ibid.* at 114A; *Gorgias* 523B, and *ibid.* at 525A; *Republic* 363DE, and *ibid.* at 614A ff.; *Theaetetus* 177A; *Laws* 870DE, and *ibid.* at 881AB; 904CD; 959A. — The statement that the philosophic life is the only free life can also be found in Plato, *Theaetetus* 173C, and *ibid.* at 175DE: ". . . the free men . . . whom we call philosopher." In *Laws* 875C, Plato maintains that the true philosopher needs neither a master nor laws to guide him: "I speak here of the intellect, true and free, and in harmony with nature." See also Aristotle, *Metaphysics* 982 b 24 ff.: "Evidently, then, we do not seek . . . [philosophic knowledge] for the sake of another advantage. But as a man is free . . . who exists for his own sake and not for the sake of another, so we pursue this [philosophic knowledge] as the only free science. For it alone exists for its own sake." See comments to fragment 47, *infra.*

— 42 —

Iamblich., *Protrep.* 53,15-54,5; frag. 58 Rose; frag. 12 Walzer; frag. 12 Ross; frag. 44 Düring. — See also Cicero,

De Finibus V. 25. 73. — In *Metaphysics* 982 b 20 ff., Aristotle states: ". . . since they pursue philosophy in order to escape from ignorance, they evidently seek knowledge in order to know rather than for any utilitarian end." — According to Heracleides of Pontus, Pythagoras defined the true "philosopher" as the "viewer of the sublime spectacle." See F. Wehrli, frag. 88 (Heracleides Ponticus); Cicero, *Tusculan Disputations* V. 3. 8-10 (who, it may be assumed, fairly accurately recounts the report of Heracleides of Pontus): "Pythagoras . . . once discussed certain matters with Leon, the ruler of the Phliasians. And Leon asked him to name the art upon which he placed the greatest reliance. But Pythagoras replied that for his part he had acquaintance with no particular art, but was merely a philosopher. Astonished by the novelty of the term, Leon asked him who these philosophers were and how they differed from the rest of mankind and the world. Pythagoras . . . replied that the life of man seemed to him to resemble the festival which was celebrated with most magnificent games before a concourse from the whole of Greece. For at this festival some men . . . sought to win the glorious distinction of a crown; others were attracted by the prospect of material gain through buying and selling. But there was yet another particular class of people, and that being quite the best type of men, who were interested neither in applauding nor seeking gain, but came for the sake of the spectacle itself and closely watched what was done and how it was done. So also we, as though we had come from some city to a crowded festival, leaving in like fashion another life and nature of being, entered upon this life, and some were slaves of ambition, others of money. But there were a special few who, counting all else for nothing, closely scanned the nature of things. These men gave themselves the name of 'lovers of wisdom' (*sapientiae studiosi* — philosophers) — and this is

the meaning of the term 'philosophers' — and just as
at the games or festivals the men of the most exalted
education look on without some self-seeking purpose, so
in life the very contemplation of things and their understanding by far surpasses all other pursuits . . ." See
also Diogenes Laertius VIII. 8 (on the authority of Sosi-
crates), and *ibid.* at I. 12; Iamblichus, *Vita Pythagorae*
pp. 58 ff.; Alexis, *Tarentinoi*, in: Athenaeus, *Deipnoso-
phistae* XI. 463DE. — From all this it would follow
that perhaps Aristotle (in the *Protrepticus*; rather than
Heracleides of Pontus, as is usually claimed) is the first
to use the panegyric-analogy. Aristotle, *Nicomachean
Ethics* 1099 a 3, by referring to the Olympic Games,
and St. Paul, *I Corinthians* 9:24, by referring to the
Isthmian Games, likewise make use of the panegyric-
analogy. — The notion of "viewing the sublime spectacle"
(or, vision — *theoria*), which in all likelihood goes back
to Plato, would suggest, however, that Pythagoras should
have called himself a "lover of the sublime vision" (*philo-
theamon*) rather than a philosopher (*philosophos*). — The
story that the term "philosopher" was first coined or first
used by Pythagoras might not stand up under close scru-
tiny. Anaxagoras is said to have stated that he had been
born to the end "to contemplate" (Diogenes Laertius II.
10), and Democritus is reported to have maintained that
"the great joys are derived from the vision of beautiful
(or, perfect) things." Diels-Kranz, *Die Fragmente der
Vorsokratiker,* vol. 2 (1935), p. 185, lines 15-16 (frag.
B 104). In brief, according to these definitions philosophy
is a sort of "beatific vision." — The notion of the "nature and reality (or, truth) of things," is also expressed
in Plato, *Theaetetus* 173E-174A: "[The philospher's] mind
. . . interrogates the whole nature of each and all [things]
in their entirety."

— 43 —

Iamblich., *Protrep.* 54,10-22; frag. 13 Walzer; frag. 13
Ross; frag. 46 Düring. — Analogies between the philosopher
and the physician are rather common with Plato who,
it appears, had a high opinion of the latter. See, for
instance, Plato, *Statesman* 293B ff., and *ibid.* at 295B ff.;
296BC, where he compares the art of the true statesman with that of the true physician, though for an entirely different purpose than, for instance, Aristotle in
the *Protrepticus.* See here also Aristotle, *Nicomachean
Ethics* 1102 a 17 ff. See also Plato, *Charmides* 156BC.

— 44 —

Iamblich., *Protrep.* 54,22-55,6; frag. 13 Walzer; frag. 13
Ross; frag. 47 Düring. — See also Ioannis Philoponus,
Comment. in Categ., CIAG XIII, 2 (A. Busse), p. 4,34-
35; Proclus, *Comment. in Primum Euclidis Elementorum
Librum* (G. Friedlein), p. 39,20-40,2. — Compare here
Plato, *Philebus* 56B ff.: "The art of the (house-) builder
. . . which makes use of a number of measures and
instruments, achieves through these instruments a greater degree of accuracy than do the other arts . . . In
ship-building and house-building . . . the builder has
his rule, lathe, compass, line . . . This being so, let us
subdivide the arts (or crafts) . . . into two kinds: the
arts which, like music, are less exact in their results, and
those arts, which like the carpenter's art, are more exact. [And of the more exact arts] one is popular [empiri-
cal ?, applied ?] and the other philsophical [purely theoretical ?]." See also Plato, *Cratylus* 389A, and Aristotle,
Eudemian Ethics 1249 a 21 ff.: "Since the physician has
a standard by reference to which he distinguishes the
healthy body from the unhealthy body, and with reference to which each thing . . . ought to be done and is

appropriate, while if less is done health can no longer
be guaranteed, so also in regard to actions and choice of
what is naturally good but not praiseworthy, the good
man should have a standard . . ." *Ibid.* at 1222 b 7 ff. —
The idea that we derive, or can derive, some of our
tools from nature — a notion already advanced by Democritus — can also be found in *De Caelo* 268 a 13 ff., where
Aristotle points out that we take the three dimensions
from nature. See in this connection also the interesting
passage in Aristotle, *Physics* 199 b 28 ff.: "'If the art
of ship-building were in the wood, it would produce the
same results by nature. If, therefore, purpose is present
in art it is present also in nature." The idea that the
statesman must have some directives that are derived
from nature in order to govern properly, also appears in
Plato, *Republic* 500B ff.; *Laws* 962B ff.

— 45 —

Iamblich., *Protrep.* 55,6-14; frag. 13 Walzer; frag. 13
Ross; frag. 48 Düring. — See also Plutarch, *De Virtute
Morali* 5. 443F; Stobaeus, *Eclogues* I. 48. 6 (p. 316,
K. Wachsmuth). — Plato insists that "no one who has
not studied philosophy . . . is permitted to enter the
company of the gods" (*Phaedo* 82B), that is, can possess
objective knowledge or knowledge of the first principles
which are necessary to govern cities. See here *Republic,
passim; Statesman, passim;* especially *ibid.* at 293A-301E;
Laws, passim; etc. In *Cratylus* 436A ff., Plato insists
that reliance on knowledge derived "from second hand"
(from experience) rather than from first hand (Ideas)
leads to "inaccuracy" and "error." See also *Timaeus* 50C
ff., and *ibid.* at 51A ff. Plato also maintains that "the
philosopher is a lover, not of a part of wisdom, but
only of the whole of wisdom" (*Republic* 475B, see also
Phaedo 91A; and *Sophist* 254A); that "philosophical

minds always have knowledge of a sort which shows
them the eternal nature" (*Republic* 485C; see also *ibid.*
at 486DE; and *Sophist* 249CD); that "the philosophers
alone are able to grasp the eternal and unchangeable"
(*Republic* 484B); that the "philosopher's eye is ever directed towards things immutable and fixed: . . . these
he imitates, and to those he will, as far as this is possible,
conform" (*Republic* 500BC); and that "by doing away
with the Ideas of things" and by denying "that every
individual thing has its own determinate Idea which is
always one and the same, [we] will have nothing on
which the mind can rest . . ." (*Parmenides* 135BC).
— See here also Aristotle, *Metaphysics* 982 a 23 ff.: "Of
those things, the most universal are on the whole the
most difficult to know, for they are farthest away from
the senses. And the most exact of the sciences are those
which deal most with first principles." But Plato, in *Republic* 409B, admits that a good judge should also have
learned from experience and observation. Aristotle, in
Nicomachean Ethics 1181 b 2, points out that "even physicians do not seem to be made solely by the study of
text-books [*scil.*, theory]." *Ibid.* at 1098 a 29, Aristotle states
that the carpenter investigates the right angle insofar
as the right angle is useful to his craft, while the geom-
eter investigates what sort of thing a right angle is, for
he is a spectator of the truth. See also *ibid.* at 1080 b
17. Aristotle, *De Partibus Animalium* 644 b 23 ff.

— 46 —

Iamblich., *Protrep.* 55,14-25; frag. 13 Walzer; frag. 13
Ross; frag. 49 Düring. — See here also Iamblich., *Math.
Scient.* 97,3-8. — Here Aristotle advocates the kind of
ideal ruler and lawgiver Plato had so eloquently extolled
in the *Republic*, the *Statesman*, and the *Laws*. Like
Plato, Aristotle seems to propound here the view that

there is no valid criterion of the excellence of the body
politic other than the "science" possessed by the true ruler. But while Plato insists that the true ruler and the
true lawgiver (the "philosopher king") should always
look to the Ideas for guidance and inspiration, Aristotle
recommends that the lawgiver, like the competent house-
builder, should use exact "scientific instruments" which
are constructed in accordance with the laws of physical
nature, that is, "borrowed from [experimental] nature itself." About the deficiencies inherent in all imitations
and in all experimental facts, see fragment 45, *supra,* and
the corresponding comments. Crete and Sparta were
often cited in the Academy as examples of "good" constitutions.

— 47 —

Iamblich., *Protrep.* 55, 26-56,2; frag. 13 Walzer; frag. 13
Ross; frag. 50 Düring. — Here Aristotle may be under the
influence of Plato, *Republic* 500BC, quoted in comments
to fragment 45, *supra.* — In *Statesman* 296E ff., Plato compares the pilot (or, captain) of a ship to the lawgiver:
"Just as the pilot, by watching continually over the interests of his ship and over the crew—not by laying down
rules [of navigation?], but by making his art the law—preserves the lives of his fellow-sailors, so, in the same
manner, may there not be a true form of public polity
by those who are able to govern in a similar spirit, and
who show a strength of art which is superior to law?"
See also *Republic* 488DE; *Gorgias* 511D ff.; *Statesman*
293A ff.; *Laws* 875CD. — About the man who "lives his
own life," see also Aristotle, *Nicomachean Ethics* 1128
a 31: "The refined and free man . . . is a law unto
himself." *Ibid.* at 1177 a 33 ff.: the philosopher is self-
sufficient. See comments to fragment 41, *supra.*

— 48 —

Iamblich., *Protrep.* 56,2-12; frag. 13 Walzer; frag. 13
Ross; frag. 51 Düring. — See also Plutarch, *De Sollertia
Animalium* 3 (961A, edit. D. Wyttenbach). — The main
idea is that theoretical knowledge "guides" our practical
actions. Similar notions are expressed in Plato, *Statesman*
293A ff.; *Philebus* 56BC. In *Physics* 252 a 33, Aristotle
points out that sense-perception often shows us that a
theory (hypothesis?) is incorrect. Plato, in *Republic* 352B
ff., stresses the fact that people devoid of justice (of
the Idea of justice) are incapable of doing just acts. See
also Plato, *Charmides* 174C ff.; *Laws* 660E. Aristotle, in
Posterior Analytics 99 b 35 ff., maintains that "all animals
possess a congenital discriminative capacity which is called
sense-perception. But although sense-perception is innate
in all animals, in some the sense-impression seems to
persist, while in others it does not. Thus, animals in
which this persistence does not occur have either no
knowledge at all outside the act of perceiving, or have
no knowledge of objects which they do not experience
through sense impression. Animals, in which it does
occur, have perception and can continue to retain a sense-
impression in the soul." — References to the human
eye can also be found in Plato, *Republic* 518A, and *ibid.*
at 527E; 533D; 540A; *Theaetetus* 156D; and in Aristotle, *Metaphysics* 980 a 25; *Nicomachean Ethics* 1096
b 29, and *ibid.* at 1143 b 14.

— 49 —

Iamblich., *Math. Scient.* 79, 15-80,1; frag. 52 Rose; frag.
5 Walzer; frag. 5 Ross; frag. 52 Düring. — See also
Proclus, *Comment. in Primum Euclidis Elementorum Librum* (G. Friedlein), pp. 25,12-26,15, and *ibid.* at p.
28,7-22; Cicero, *De Finibus* II. 13. 40. — This fragment,

which might not have been part of the original *Protrepticus,* to some extent implements fragment 48.

— 50 —

Iamblich., *Protrep.* 40,1-11; frag. 52 Rose; frag. 5 Walzer; frag. 5 Ross; frag. 53 Düring. — See also [Isocrates,] *Ad Demonicum* 19. — The first part of this fragment reminds us of Marcus Aurelius (XII. 6), although it is extremely doubtful that he was influenced by the *Protrepticus*: "Let . . . philosophy be thy own step-mother and mother, return to philosophy and repose in her." But then, again, it might be under the influence of the concluding sentence of Plato's *Euthydemus* 307C: "But if [philosophy] be what I believe her to be, then follow her and serve her, you and your house, as the saying goes, and be of good cheer." — In *Republic* 504DE, Plato states: "When things of little relevance are elaborated with infinite pains . . . how ridiculous that we should not think the highest truth worthy of the highest and most painstaking attention." — The idea that only vulgar persons would prefer just living to the "good life" sounds definitely Platonic. See, for instance, Plato, *Laws* 707D: ". . . the mere continuance of life is not the most honorable thing for men, as the vulgar think, but the continuance of the best life, while we live." See also Plato, *Apology* 28A, and *ibid.* at 38Eff.; *Gorgias* 511C, and *ibid.* at 522E; *Republic* 445AB; *Laws* 661A ff., and *ibid.* at 828D; 944E; *et passim.* — The notion that the vulgar man prefers to follow the opinions of the many instead of expecting the many to follow his opinion might have been influenced by Plato, *Crito* 48A: "And, therefore, you begin in error when you advise that we should pay heed to the opinions of the many about the just and the unjust, good and evil, honorable and dishonorable." See here also Aristotle, who, in *Nicomachean*

Ethics 1169 a 20 ff., insists that the good man "will throw away both wealth and honors . . . gaining for himself nobility. Because he would prefer a twelve-month period of noble life to many years of humdrum existence, and one great and noble deed to many trivial ones." *Eudemian Ethics* 1215 b 34 ff.: "Would a single man value life [above all else], unless he were utterly servile . . .?" *Metaphysics* 982 a 18 ff.: "For the wise man must not be ordered, but must order; and he must not obey another, but the less wise must obey him."

— 51 —

Iamblich., *Protrep.* 40,12-15 (see also Iamblich., *Math. Scient.* 82,14-17); frag. 52 Rose; frag. 5 Walzer; frag. 5 Ross; frag. 54 Düring. — In *Rhetoric* 1363 a 21, Aristotle insists that "things are done 'easily' when they are done without pain [and without great labor] or with much speed . . ."

— 52 —

Iamblich., *Protrep.* 40,15-20 (see also Iamblich., *Math. Scient.* 82,17-22); frag. 52 Rose; frag. 5 Walzer; frag. 5 Ross; frag. 55 Düring. — Plato, in *Theaetetus* 173C ff., maintains that "to the world the philosopher is a fool," and in *Republic* 489A ff., he insists that "philosophers have no honor in their Cities," because philosophy is "useless to the rest of the world." But this "uselessness" must be attributed to the fact that people simply refuse to resort to true philosophy. See here also *Republic* 498E ff., and *ibid.* at 500B; 489CD; *Phaedrus* 249 DE; *Euthydemus* 304D ff. — In *Republic* 487A, Plato maintains that the philosopher "has the gift of a good memory, and is quick to learn." See also *ibid.* at 503C. *Ibid.* at 528B ff., Plato complains that theoretical (speculative)

or philosophic studies do not flourish because "no government patronizes them. This situation results in a want of
interest and energy in the pursuit of them . . . Students
cannot study them unless they have a preceptor. But
then a preceptor can hardly be found, and even if he
can be found, as matters now stand, the students, who
are very conceited, would not listen to him. This situation,
however, would be entirely different if the whole City
should become the preceptor of these students and give
honor (and respectability) to . . . [theoretical and philosophic studies]."

— 53 —

Iamblich., *Protrep.* 40,20-41,2 (see also Iamblich., *Math.*
Scient. 82,22-83,2); frag. 52 Rose; frag. 5 Walzer; frag.
5 Ross; frag. 56 Düring.—See also [Isocrates,] *Ad Demoni-*
cum 46; Plutarch, *De Cupiditate Divitiarum* X. 528A
(Xylander). — Plato, in *Euthydemus* 304E, calls philso-
phy "a charming thing"; and in *Gorgias* 484C, he de-
scribes it as "an elegant accomplishment." — The notion
that truth (or beauty) is everywhere can also be
found in Plato, *Symposium* 210E ff. See here also Aristotle, *Nicomachean Ethics* 1177 a 23 ff.: "[T]he activity of
philosophic wisdom is admittedly the most pleasant of
all virtuous actions. Under all circumstances, the pursuit
of . . . [philosophic contemplation] is considered to offer
pleasures unsurpassed for their purity and their enduring
values . . . The philosopher, even when by himself, can
contemplate truth. . ." Aristotle, *Rhetoric* 1371 a 31:
"Learning things and wondering at things are also pleasant . . ." Aristotle, *Poetics* 1448 b 13 ff.: "To be learning
something is the greatest of pleasures, not only to the
philosopher, but also to the rest of mankind, however
small their capacity for it. The reason of the delight . . .
is . . . learning, the getting of the meaning of things."

— 54 —

Iamblich., *Protrep.* 41,2-5 (see also Iamblich., *Math. Scient.* 83,2-5); frag. 52 Rose; frag. 5 Walzer; frag. 5 Ross; frag. 57 Düring. — Plato, in *Phaedo* 61A, insists that philosophy is the "noblest and best of music (intellectual pursuits)."

— 55 —

Iamblich., *Protrep.* 41,15-20; frag. 6 Walzer; frag. 6 Ross; frag. 59 Düring. — There is something missing, perhaps a transitional passage, between fragment 54 and fragment 55. Düring, frag. 58, inserts the following passage of his own: "We shall now attempt to explain, by making a fresh start, what the proper function of philosophic wisdom (*phronesis*) is, and why all men strive after philosophic wisdom." — Plato, as is well known, insists that the soul is, and always must be, the supreme ruler of the body. (*Phaedo* 80A ff., and *ibid.* at 94B ff.; *Timaeus* 34C; *Laws* 726A ff.; *I Alcibiades* 130B ff.); that it uses the body for its own purposes (*Phaedo* 80A ff.); that it is infinitely superior to the body (*Laws* 892A ff., and *ibid.* at 959A); that it is prior to the body (*Laws* 726A, and *ibid.* at 728AB; 966DE; *et passim*); that the body is inferior to the soul (*Laws* 728D ff., and *ibid.* at 743E; 892A); and that the body exists for the sake of the soul (*Laws* 870B).

— 56 —

Iamblich., *Protrep.* 41,20-24; frag. 6 Walzer; frag. 6 Ross; frag. 60 Düring. — The idea of the "proper balance of the soul" is discussed in Plato, *Republic* 352A ff. The notion that in the soul there are two parts, one which rules and one which is ruled, is also found in Aristotle,

Magna Moralia 1206 b 17-29, and *ibid.* at 1206 b 9-14.
In *Eudemian Ethics* 1220 a 2 ff., Aristotle insists that
"just as the generally good condition of a body is com-
pounded of the partial excellences, so also the excellences
of the soul, in accordance with its end." See also *ibid.*
at 1220 a 5 ff., where Aristotle maintains that the rational part of the soul "governs the soul by possessing
reason," and that the moral part of the soul is "by its
nature obedient to the part which possesses reason." —
In *Physics* 246 a 13 ff., and in *Metaphysics* 1021 b 20-30,
Aristotle proclaims that "excellence is a perfection," and
that each thing is complete (or perfect) when it lacks
nothing proper to it.

– 57 –

Iamblich., *Protrep.* 41,24-42,1; frag. 6 Walzer; frag. 6
Ross; frag. 61 Düring. — The notion that the perfect order is achieved whenever the best, the most authoritative,
and the most honorable parts are in control is definitely
Platonic. In the domain of political thought this notion
is expressed many times in the *Republic*, the *Statesman*,
and the *Laws*, as well as in other dialogues. See, for
example, *Republic* 431A. — The idea that "what is naturally better is also morally better," is likewise Platonic.
It is restated in Aristotle, *Politics* 1323 b 13 ff., and
Eudemian Ethics 1219 a 6. See also *Magna Moralia* 1208
a 9 ff.: "To act, then, in accordance with right reason
is to prevent the irrational part of the soul from interfer-
ing with the rational part, in the exercising of its proper
function. For only then will the action be in accordance
with right reason. For seeing that in the soul we have
'a something worse' and 'a something better,' and the
worse is always for the sake of the better, as in the
case of body and soul where the body is for the sake
of the soul, and then only shall we say that we have

our body in a good state, when its state is such as not
to hinder, but actually to help and partake in inciting
the soul to accomplish its own work. . ." — Although
Plato had spoken of a tripartite soul (*Republic* 435B ff.;
Phaedrus 246A ff.; *Timaeus* 69C ff.), there can be de-
tected in his later writings a definite tendency to stress
a sort of bipartite soul by identifying the "courageous"
part and the "appetitive" part. Thus, in *Republic* 608D
ff., he distinguishes between the "rational" part and the
other parts of the soul, claiming that only the former
is immortal; and in *Timaeus* 65A, and *ibid.* at 72D, he
admits that the division into the rational part and the
irrational parts of the soul is the more important division.
See also *Statesman* 309C and *Laws* 863B, as well as
Aristotle, *Magna Moralia* 1182 a 23 ff.: "After this Plato
divided the soul into the rational and the irrational part."
— Aristotle likewise divides the soul into (two) parts.
See, for instance, *Eudemian Ethics* 1219 b 26, and *ibid.*
at 1220 a 2; 1220 b 5-6; 1221 b 27-34; 1246 a 26 ff.;
Nicomachean Ethics 1102 a 23 ff., and *ibid.* at 1138
b 5 ff.; 1138 b 25 ff.; 1143 b 14ff.; 1144 a 1 ff.; 1145
a 11; 1168 b 19 ff.; *Politics* 1254 a 24 ff., and *ibid.*
at 1277 a 5 ff.; 1332 a 38 ff.; 1333 a 16 ff.; *Rhetoric*
1368 b 37 ff., and *ibid.* at 1370 a 18 ff.

— 58 —

Iamblich., *Protrep.* 41,1-4; frag. 6 Walzer; frag. 6 Ross;
frag. 62 Düring. — In *Republic* 353B ff., Plato maintains
that "that to which an end is appointed has an excellence," and that "of all things (other things), they, each
of them, [have] an end and a special excellence . . . and
the soul, has it not an excellence of its own also?" Then
Plato goes on, stating that the excellence of the soul
is the most exalted excellence. See also Plato, *Republic*
443D: ". . . the inward man . . . is the true self and the

foremost concern of man . . ." See also Plato, *Laws* 959A:
". . . even in this life what makes each one of us to be
what we are is only the soul. . . ." *I Alcibiades* 130C,
where Plato states that the soul as such is man. —
Aristotle, in *Nicomachean Ethics* 1177 b 34 ff., insists
that we must always live "in accordance with the best
things in us." This implies that above all we must be
ourselves, our best self, since the latter "is the authoritative and better part of man. It would be strange, then,
if we were to choose not the life of the 'self,' but that
of something else . . . [T]hat which is proper to each
thing is by nature best . . . for each thing. For man,
therefore, the life according to reason is best . . . since
reason more than anything else is man."

— 59 —

Iamblich., *Protrep.* 42,5-9; frag. 6 Walzer; frag. 6 Ross;
frag. 63 Düring. — See here fragment 58, *supra,* and the
corresponding comments. — In *Eudemian Ethics* 1219 a
18 ff., Aristotle points out that "the [good] work of a
thing is also the work of its excellence . . ."; and in
Nicomachean Ethics 1106 a 15 ff., he insists that "every
virtue or excellence brings into good condition the thing
of which it is the excellence, and makes the work of
that thing be done well. . . ." Similar notions are also
expressed in Plato, *Republic* 352D ff. — See also Aristotle, *Metaphysics* 1021 b 20 ff.; *Physics* 246 a 13 ff.,
mentioned in comments to fragment 56, *supra.*

— 60 —

Iamblich., *Protrep.* 42,9-13; frag. 6 Walzer; frag. 6 Ross;
frag. 64 Düring. — The idea expressed here is akin to
what Plato says in the *Phaedrus* 270DE: "When we are
considering nature, ought we not to consider first whether

that which we want to know is simple or composite. If
it is simple, then we ought to investigate the power
it possesses of acting or being acted upon in relation
to other things; and if it is composite, then [we ought]
to enumerate the forms, and then, in the case of all of
them, [investigate] what is the power of acting or being
acted upon that makes each and everyone of them to
be what they are."

— 61 —

Iamblich., *Protrep.* 42,13-23; frag. 6 Walzer; frag. 0 Ross;
frag. 65 Düring. — See also Cicero, *Hortensius*, frag. 101
Müller (St. Augustine, *Contra Academicos* I. 3. 7). —
Aristotle seems to imply here that a working harmony
must exist, or be established, between the rational and
the irrational parts of the soul. See, for instance, Aristotle, *Nicomachean Ethics* 1139 b 12 ff., where he states
that "the work of both the intellectual parts [of the soul]
is truth. Hence, the states that are most strictly those in
respect of which each of these two parts will attain
truth are the respective virtues of the two parts." See
also *ibid.* at 1139 a 21 ff. The notion of a working harmony between the rational and irrational parts of the
soul is amplified in Aristotle, *Magna Moralia* 1200 a 2 ff.:
"As soon as one is faced by a choice, perfect virtue
will be present . . . accompanied by wisdom, but not
without the natural impulse to do the right thing. Nor
will one virtue run counter to another, for its nature is
to obey the dictates of reason, so that it inclines toward
that to which reason leads. For it is this which chooses
better. For the other virtues do not come into existence
without wisdom, nor is wisdom perfect without the other
virtues. But they co-operate with one another, in a sense,
by attending upon wisdom." — See also comments to fragment 21, *supra,* and comments to fragment 89, *infra.*

— 62 —

Iamblich., *Protrep.* 42,23-29; frag. 6 Walzer; frag. 6
Ross; frag. 66 Düring. — Here Aristotle asks the basic question: How can we attain to truth? His answer: Through
the acquisition of knowledge (or of first principles?).
And the ultimate end of all forms of knowledge is philosophic knowledge (*theoria*). The term *theoria*, which
actually signifies "objective vision of the sublime truth,"
is essentially Platonic. See comments to fragment 42,
supra.

— 63 —

Iamblich., *Protrep.* 43,1-5; frag. 6 Walzer; frag. 6 Ross;
frag. 67 Düring. — Aristotle's assertion that the rational
(or cognitive) part of the soul (or, reason, *nous*) —
whether by itself or in combination with other parts of
the soul — is superior to all other parts of the soul, and
that knowledge is the excellence of the soul, is probably
under the influence of Plato, *Protagoras* 352A ff.; *Euthydemus* 292B; and *Timaeus* 90A ff. In the *Statesman*
259A ff., Plato insists that "the royal knowledge is a
commanding type," using subordinate instrumentalities
and ruling over "compounds" or "collective" entities as
"individuals." See here also Aristotle, *Nicomachean Ethics* 1097 b 31.

— 64 —

Iamblich., *Protrep.* 43,5-14; frag. 6 Walzer; frag. 6 Ross;
frag. 68 Düring. — Aristotle refers here to the four cardinal virtues of Plato. See Plato, *Republic* 428A ff., and
ibid. at 433B; *Laws* 631CD, and *ibid.* at 688AD; 965CD;
etc. The moral virtues are subordinated to the *phronesis.*
— The notion that philosophic knowledge must be productive can also be found in Plato, *Euthydemus* 292D:
". . . the knowledge by which we are to make other

men good. . . and these others will make good others . . ."
See here Aristotle, *Magna Moralia* 1200 a 7 ff.: "For
it is this [*scil.*, wisdom] which chooses . . . The other virtues do not come into existence without wisdom, nor is
wisdom perfect without the other virtues." See also *ibid.*
at 1185 b 5 ff.: "[In the rational part of the soul], then,
there reside wisdom, readiness of wit, philosophy, aptitude to learn, memory, and so forth. But in the irrational
part [of the soul] reside those which are called the virtues,
namely, temperance, justice, courage, and such other
moral states as are held to be praiseworthy." — Aristotle
holds that the science of doing some things is not part
of the result achieved by this science; and that the
purpose of science is knowledge rather than production.
See, for instance, Aristotle, *Physics* 200 a 24: "Only the
starting point of the reasoning is in [pure] mathematics,
as there is no production." *Metaphysics* 1013 b 6; *Eudemian Ethics* 1216 b 10 ff.: "[To inquire what virtue is,
not how or from what it arises] is correct with regard
to theoretical knowledge . . . though nothing prevents
them from being in an accidental way useful to us. But
the end of the practical or productive sciences is different from [pure] science and knowledge, as for instance,
health [is different] from medical science. . . ."

— 65 —

Iamblich., *Protrep.* 43,14-20; frag. 6 Walzer; frag. 6 Ross;
frag. 69 Düring. — Final cause or purpose is frequently
defined by Aristotle as "that for the sake of which."
See, for instance, *Physics* 194 a 27, and *ibid.* at 200 a
22; 200 a 34; *Metaphysics* 1013 a 33; etc.

— 66 —

Iamblich., *Protrep.* 43,20-25; frag. 6 Walzer; frag. 6 Ross;

frag. 70 Düring. — Like Plato's, Aristotle's view is that philosophy and philosophic contemplation are the sources of man's greatest happiness. See *Nicomachean Ethics* 1177 a 11 ff.; *Politics* 1324 a 28; etc. — Plato likewise extolls sight. See, for instance, *Republic* 507C ff., and *ibid.* at 508A ff.; 532A; *Theaetetus* 163B ff.; *Timaeus* 47A ff.: "Sight . . . is the source of the greatest benefit to us . . . [It] has given us the power of inquiring about the nature of the universe, and from this source we have derived philosophy . . . God invented and gave us sight to the end that we might behold the courses of intelligence in the heavens. . ." Aristotle maintains that sight gives us more knowledge than any of the other senses. See, for instance, *Metaphysics* 980 a 21 ff., quoted in comments to fragment 68, *infra.*

— 67 —

Iamblich., *Protrep.* 43,27-44,9; frag. 7 Walzer; frag. 7 Ross; frag. 71 Düring. — The contrast of "true opinion" and "philosophic insight" is definitely Platonic, as is the notion that "philosophic insight" is superior to "true opinion." See, for instance, *Republic* 509D ff. — In *Politics* 1323 b 13 ff., Aristotle points out that "the best state of one thing in relation to another thing corresponds in degree of excellence to the difference between the natures of which we say that these very states are states; so that, if the soul is more excellent than our earthly possessions or our bodies, both absolutely and in relation to us, it must be conceded that the best state of either has a similar ratio to the other."

— 68 —

Iamblich., *Protrep.* 43,25-27; frag. 7 Walzer; frag. 7 Ross; frag. 72 Düring. — In *Metaphysics* 980 a 21 ff., Aristotle states: "All men by nature desire (or love) to know.

An indication of this is the delight which we take in our senses. For even apart from their usefulness they are loved for themselves; and above all others the sense of sight. For not only with a view to action, but even when we are not going to do anything, we prefer seeing . . . to everything else. The reason is that this, more than any other sense, makes us know and brings to light many differences between things." Some scholars insist that fragment 68 of the *Protrepticus* is but an abbreviated rendition of *Metaphysics* 980 a 21 ff. It is held that *Metaphysics*, books A and B (and 980 a 21 ff. is part of book A), at least in their earliest version, and the *Protrepticus* were written at approximately the same time.

— 69 —

Iamblich., *Protrep.* 44,9-13; frag. 7 Walzer; frag. 7 Ross; frag. 74 Düring. — I. Düring, *op. cit.*, at pp. 242-243, suggests that in *Eudemian Ethics* 1244 b 26 ff. Aristotle comments on this particular fragment: "Mere perception and mere knowledge are more desirable to every man, and, hence, the desire of living is congenital in all men. For living must be regarded as a kind of knowledge. If, then, we were to cut off and abstract mere knowledge and its opposite—this passes unnoticed in the argument as we have given it [in the *Protrepticus*?], but in fact it need not remain unnoticed—there would be no difference between this and another's knowing instead of oneself. And this is like another's living instead of oneself. But naturally the perception and knowledge of oneself is more desirable. For we must take two things into consideration, namely, that life is something desirable and also the 'good'; and, hence, that it is desirable that such a nature should belong to oneself . . . [T]o wish to perceive oneself is to wish oneself to be of a certain character . . . by participation in these qualities in perceiving and know-

ing. For the perceiver becomes perceived in that way
and in that respect in which he first perceives, and
according to the way in which—and according to the
object which—he perceives. And the knower becomes
known in the same way. Hence, it is for this reason
that one always desires to live, because one always
desires to know. And this is because he himself wishes
to be the object known."

— 70 —

Iamblich., *Protrep.* 44,13-17; frag. 7 Walzer; frag. 7
Ross; frag. 75 Düring. — See here the comments to fragment 66, *supra.* — Plato, in *Theaetetus* 184C, points out
that we hear "through" our ears rather than "with" our
ears.

— 71 —

Iamblich., *Protrep.* 44,17-20; frag. 7 Walzer; frag. 7
Ross; frag. 76 Düring. — This passage has a familiar ring.
Plato, in *Republic* 532A ff., maintains that dialectic "is
that strain which is of the intellect only, but which the
faculty of sight will nevertheless be found to imitate.
For sight . . . was imagined by us after a while to behold
the real animals and stars, and last of all, the sun itself.
And so with dialectic: when a person starts on the dis-
covery of the absolute by the light of reason only, and
without any assistance by the senses, and perseveres until
by pure intelligence (or, pure reason) he arrives at the
perception of the absolute good, he at last finds himself
at the end of the intellectual world, as in the case of
sight at the end of the visible."

— 72 —

Iamblich., *Protrep.* 44,20-26; frag. 7 Walzer; frag. 7

Ross; frag. 77 Düring. — Plato, in *Apology* 28A, and *ibid.* at 38A; *Gorgias* 511B ff., and *ibid.* at 522DE; and *Laws* 828D, and *ibid.* at 831AB; 944C, insists that life is not to be preferred under all circumstances; in *Crito* 48B ff.; *Laws* 661BC, and *ibid.* at 707CD; 727D; *Republic* 445A, that life is valuable only when good; and in *Laws* 862E, that life is without value to the bad man. — See here also Plato's argument in the *Euthydemus* 282A: "Seeing that all men desire happiness, and happiness . . . is gained by the use—the right use—of the things of life, and the right use of them, and good fortune in the use of them, is given by knowledge—the inference is that every one by all means ought to try to make himself as wise as possible." See also Aristotle, *Eudemian Ethics* 1246 b 32: ". . . prudence and virtue go together . . ."

— 73 —

Iamblich., *Protrep.* 44,26-45,3; frag. 7 Walzer; frag. 7 Ross; frag. 73 Düring. — See comments to fragments 66, 67, and 68, *supra*.

— 74 —

Iamblich., *Protrep.* 56,13-15; frag. 14 Walzer; frag. 14 Ross; frag. 78 Düring. — Plato, in *I Alcibiades* 134A ff., stresses the fact that only the wise man can be happy. See also Plato, *Charmides* 173AB ff.; *Meno* 88CD; *Republic* 580B ff., especially *ibid.* at 583A: ". . . the wise man speaks with authority when he approves of his own life." Aristotle, in *Nicomachean Ethics* 1178 a 6 ff., maintains that "the life according to reason is best and most pleasant, since reason more than anything else is man. This life, therefore, is also the happiest."

— 75 —

Iamblich., *Protrep.* 56,15-22; frag. 14 Walzer; frag. 14
Ross; frag. 79 Düring. — Plato, in *Theaetetus* 197B ff., distinguishes between "to know" and "to possess knowledge."
See also *ibid.* at 199A ff. As a matter of fact, the argument made by Aristotle in fragment 75 is very similar
to that advanced by Plato in *Theaetetus* 197B ff., and
ibid. at 199A ff.

— 76 —

Iamblich., *Protrep.* 56,22-57,7; frag. 14 Walzer; frag. 14
Ross; frag. 80 Düring. — Similar notions are expressed in
Aristotle, *Eudemian Ethics* 1244 b 23 ff.: "It will be clear
if we ascertain what life is in its active sense and in its
end. Clearly, it is perception and knowledge." See comments to fragment 69, *supra.* — See also Plato, *Theaetetus*
158B ff., where he discusses the problem of how, when
awake, we can determine that we are not sleeping, and
vice versa. It is possible that in *Metaphysics* 1011 a 3
ff., Aristotle answers Plato's query when he maintains
that certain people demand that a reason shall be given
to everything, including the question of whether we are
now asleep or awake. — It should be noticed that in fragment 76 Aristotle uses the *potentia-actus* doctrine which
became quite basic for his whole philosophical system.
He elaborates this doctrine in detail in *Metaphysics* 1049
b 3 ff., and summarizes it *ibid.* at 1051 a 4 ff.

— 77 —

Iamblich., *Protrep.* 57,7-12; frag. 14 Walzer; frag. 14
Ross; frag. 81 Düring. — See also comments to fragment
72, *supra.* — Aristotle touches here again on the *potentia-
actus* problem. See comments to fragment 76, *supra.*

— 78 —

Iamblich., *Protrep.* 57,12-19; frag. 14 Walzer; frag. 14
Ross; frag. 82 Düring. — Essentially the same argument
is in Plato, *Philebus* 53A ff.: "How can there be purity
in whiteness, and what purity? Is that purest which is
greatest or most in quantity, or that which is most unadulterated and least affected by any admixture of other col-
ors? Clearly that which is most unadulterated . . . [T]he
purest white, and not the greatest or largest in quantity,
is to be deemed truest and most beautiful . . . And
we shall be quite right in saying that a little pure white
is whiter and fairer and truer than a great deal of white
which contains admixtures."

—79—

Iamblich., *Protrep.* 57,19-23; frag. 14 Walzer; frag. 14
Ross; frag. 83 Düring. — See also fragment 76, *supra*,
and the corresponding comments. — In Plato, *Theaetetus*
157E ff., we are told that a waking man has more true
knowledge than a sleeping man. See also *ibid.* at 197B-
198B. In *Republic* 352D ff., Plato implies that the end
of everything consists in its proper use (not merely in
possessing it). See also Aristotle, *Eudemian Ethics* 1216
a 3 ff.: "What is the difference between sleeping an un-
broken sleep from one's first day . . . and having the
life of a plant? Plants at any rate seem to possess this
sort of existence, and similarly children . . . in their
mother's womb . . ." *Magna Moralia* 1185 a 10 ff.:
"For supposing someone to be asleep all his life, we
should hardly consent to call him happy. Life he certainly has, but life in accordance with the virtues he does
not have . . ." *Ibid.* at 1201 b 15 ff.: "When man does
not operate with his knowledge, it is not surprising that
he should do what is evil, though he possess the knowl-

edge. For the case is the same as that of sleepers. Although they possess knowledge, nevertheless in their sleep they perpetrate and suffer many abominable things. For the knowledge is not operative in them." *Nicomachean Ethics* 1095 b 32 ff.: "The possession of virtue [without practical implementation] seems actually compatible with sleep, or with life-long inactivity . . . But a man living thus would not be called happy by any one . . ."

— 80 —

Iamblich., *Protrep.* 57,23-58,3; frag. 14 Walzer; frag. 14 Ross; frag. 84 Düring. — In *Euthydemus* 289D, Plato insists that "the art of making speeches is not the same as the art of using them." See also *Republic* 601C ff.; *Cratylus* 390A ff. Aristotle, in *Nicomachean Ethics* 1097 a 25 ff., states: "Since there are evidently more than just one end, and we choose one of these (such as wealth, flutes, and the general instruments) for the sake of something else, clearly not all ends are final ends. But the chief good is evidently something final. Therefore, if there were but one final end, this would be what we are seeking, and if there were more than one end, the most final of these would be that which we are seeking."

— 81 —

Iamblich., *Protrep.* 58,3-10; frag. 14 Walzer; frag. 14 Ross; frag. 85 Düring. — See fragment 66, *supra,* and the corresponding comments. — The notion that the perfect life belongs to those who think rationally and indulge in speculative philosophy is both Platonic and Aristotelian. It is expressed in Plato, *Republic* 582A ff., where we are told that life dedicated to speculative philosophy is the most perfect life. See also Plato, *Laws*

733E; *et passim.* Similar views are found in Aristotle,
Eudemian Ethics 1219 a 35 ff., where Aristotle insists that
"since happiness is something complete, and living is
either complete or incomplete and so also true virtue—
one virtue being a whole, the other a part—and the activity of what is incomplete is itself incomplete, therefore happiness would be the activity of a complete life
in accordance with complete virtue." See here also Aristotle, *Nicomachean Ethics* 1100 b 11 ff., and *ibid.* at
1177 b 26 ff.

— 82 —

Iamblich., *Protrep.* 58,10-14; frag. 14 Walzer; frag. 14
Ross; frag. 86 Düring. — Plato, in *Phaedo* 83A ff., ad-
vances the idea that the philosopher, living the most
perfect life, is "most real." Similar notions can also be
found in Plato's other works, whenever he extolls the
sublimity of the philosophic life. Since the philosophic
life is always the best life—and since the greatest goodness is also the most real reality—philosophic life must
be the most real life and, hence, the only life worth
living. See, for instance, Plato, *Phaedo* 82B ff.; *Republic*
500B ff.; *Phaedrus* 249BC; *Philebus* 28C; *Theaetetus*
176B; *Sophist* 216BC; etc. In *Republic* 582C, Plato
points out that "the delight which is to be found in the
knowledge of true being is known to the philosopher
alone." — In *Nicomachean Ethics* 1170 a 28 ff., Aristotle
says: "And if he who perceives that he sees . . . there
is something which perceives that we are active, so that
if we perceive, we perceive that we perceive; and if
we think, that we think. And to perceive that we perceive (or think) is to perceive that we exist (for existence was defined as perceiving or thinking). And if perceiving that one lives is in itself one of the things that
are pleasant (for life is by nature good, and to perceive

what is good to be present in oneself is itself pleasant);
and if life is desirable, and particularly desirable for
good men, because to them existence is good and pleasant (in that they are pleased at realizing that which
is in itself pleasant is present in man) . . . — if all this
be true . . . his own being is desirable for each man . . ."
See also *ibid.* at 1179 a 22 ff.: "Now he who exercises
his reason and cultivates it seems to be both in the best
state of mind and most dear to the gods. For if the gods
have any care of human affairs . . . it would be reasonable both that they should delight in that which is best
and most akin to them [*scil.*, reason] . . . And that all
these attributes belong most of all to the philosophers
is plainly manifest. He [*scil.*, the philosopher], therefore,
is dearest to the gods . . . and presumably also the
happiest man . . ." See also comments to fragment 104,
infra; Aristotle, *Eudemian Ethics* 1229 a 40 ff.; *Magna
Moralia* 1191 a 31 ff.; Plato, *Laws* 902C: "It would not
be natural for the gods, who own us and are the most
careful and best of owners, to neglect us." *Republic*
613AB, quoted in comments to fragment 105, *infra.*

— 83 —

Iamblich., *Protrep.* 58,15-17; frag. 14 Walzer; frag. 14
Ross; frag. 87 Düring. — In *Phaedo* 65A, Plato maintains
that the body is a hindrance to the acquisition of knowledge, and that "thought seems to be best when the
mind is gathered into itself" and not troubled by the
senses. *Ibid.* at 66B, Plato states that "the body is the
source of endless trouble," impeding us in our search
after absolute being and absolute truth. Plato, *Phaedrus*
237DE ff., and *ibid.* at 246A ff.; *Philebus* 21A ff., where
he points out that the intellectual life procures the greatest delight. See also *Republic* 582E ff. Aristotle likewise states that the absolute good in itself is pleasure.

Eudemian Ethics 1237 a 27. And in *Nicomachean Ethics* 1099 a 15 ff., he maintains that the truly philosophic or contemplative life "has its own pleasure in itself."

— 84 —

Iamblich., *Protrep.* 58,17-27; frag. 14 Walzer; frag. 14 Ross; frag. 88 Düring. — Obviously, unlike Plato, Aristotle does not take a dim view of pleasure. As a matter of fact, pleasure plays an important role in his moral philosophy: it is a "positive good." See, for instance, *Nicomachean Ethics* 1095 b 19 ff., and *ibid.* at 1172 a 9 ff.; 1153 b 4; etc. See also *ibid.* at 1152 b 26 ff. In *Magna Moralia* 1206 a 9 ff., Aristotle insists that pleasure can be an incentive to increased (worthwhile) action.

— 85 —

Iamblich., *Protrep.* 58,27-59,3; frag. 14 Walzer; frag. 14 Ross; frag. 89 Düring. — See here also fragment 84, *supra,* and the corresponding comments. — In *Eudemian Ethics* 1244 b 27, Aristotle maintains that "the desire of living is congenital in all men." See also *Politics* 1278 b 29: "Men cling to life even at the cost of enduring great misfortune, and apparently find in life a natural sweetness and happiness." In *Nicomachean Ethics* 1175 a 18 ff., he states, perhaps with Plato's rigorism in mind: "But whether we choose life for the sake of pleasure, or pleasure for the sake of life, is a question we may dismiss here. For they seem to be bound up together and do not admit of separation . . ." *Ibid.* at 1175 a 10 ff.: ". . . all men desire pleasure because they desire life. . ."

— 86 —

Iamblich., *Protrep.* 59,3-7; frag. 14 Walzer; frag. 14 Ross;

frag. 90 Düring. — Similar views can be found in Aristotle, *Eudemian Ethics* 1215 a 15 ff. In *Nicomachean
Ethics* 1098 a 7 ff., Aristotle insists that the activity of
the soul is the proper function of man, and that the activity of the soul is the true human good and, hence,
the most pleasant thing. See also *ibid.* at 1099 a 7 ff.;
and comments to fragment 83, *supra*.

— 87 —

Iamblich., *Protrep.* 59,7-17; frag. 14 Walzer; frag. 14
Ross; frag. 91 Düring. — See also Epicurus, *Epistola ad
Menoeceum* (Diogenes Laertius X. 132); Cicero, *De
Finibus* I. 13. 44. — It is possible that Aristotle alludes
here to Plato, *Republic* 586A: "Those people, then, who
know no wisdom and virtue, and who are always busy
with gluttony and sensuality, go down and up again
as far as the mean; and in this region they move at
random throughout life, but they never pass into the
true upper world [of the intellect]. Thither they never
look, nor do they find their way, neither are they filled
with true being, nor do they taste the pure and abiding
pleasure. [They are like cattle . . .]." — See here also
Aristotle, *Nicomachean Ethics* 1174 a 20 ff.: "For while
there is pleasure in respect to any sense, and in respect
of intellectual activity and contemplation no less, the most
complete is the most pleasant." *Ibid.* at 1177 a 19 ff.:
"For, in the first place, this activity [*scil.*, intellectual
thought and contemplation] is the best . . .; and, in the
second place, it is the most permanent, since we can
contemplate truth more permanently than we can do
anything else." See also *ibid.* at 1100 b 18 ff., where
Aristotle insists that permanency will belong to the happy
man who engaged in virtuous action and intellectual
contemplation.

— 88 —

Iamblich., *Protrep.* 59,17-18; frag. 14 Walzer; frag. 14 Ross; frag. 92 Düring. — The meaning of this passage is rather obvious: there is nothing wrong with enjoying the right pleasures; the practice of philosophy is the best of pleasures; hence, if one intends to enjoy real pleasures, one ought to practice philosophy above all other things. See here also *Nicomachean Ethics* 1153 a 29, and *ibid.* at 1152 b 26 ff.: Some pleasures are good. *Ibid.* at 1153 a 35 ff.: The wise man avoids pleasures that are not good, because he has pleasures of his own, namely, intellectual pleasures. *Ibid.* at 1176 a 16 ff.: If the good man (the "philosophic man") is the measure of all things, "those also will be [true] pleasures which appear to him to be such, and those things pleasant which he enjoys [namely, the practice of philosophy]." Plato had already insisted that the true philosopher is the "measure of all things." See, for instance, *Theaetetus* 166D, and *ibid.* at 168B ff.; 170C ff.; 178B; 183B; *Laws* 716CD, and *ibid.* at 875CD.

— 89 —

Iamblich., *Protrep.* 59,19-26; frag. 15 Walzer; frag. 15 Ross; frag. 93 Düring. — In *Politics* 1323 a 24 ff., Aristotle speaks of three kinds of good (see also Plato, *Laws* 697B, and *ibid.* at 743DE), namely, external (material) goods, goods of the body, and goods of the soul. The truly happy man must have all three. True happiness is more often found with those who are most cultivated in their minds and in their character. Whereas external goods have a limit, every good of the soul, the greater it is, is also of greater usefulness (and productive of greater happiness). The soul is more noble than any of the worldly possessions or our bodies. It is for the

sake of the soul that external goods and the goods of the
body may be chosen, and wise men ought to choose them
for the sake of the soul and not the soul for the sake
of the external or bodily goods. See also *Nicomachean
Ethics* 1099 a 31 ff.: "Yet evidently . . . [happiness]
needs the external goods as well. For it is impossible,
or not easy, to do noble things without the proper equip-
ment." — In all likelihood it is from Plato's *Republic*
that Aristotle borrows the notion that something composed of parts also has an excellence of its own, provided
that each component part performs its function properly.

— 90 —

Iamblich., *Protrep.* 59,26-60,1; frag. 14 Walzer; frag. 14
Ross; frag. 94 Düring. — Similar views are expressed by
Aristotle in *Eudemian Ethics* 1214 a 30 ff.: "Now happiness . . . must consist mainly of three things which
seem to be most desirable: some say philosophical knowledge (*phronesis*) is the greatest good, some virtue, and
some pleasure." See also *Magna Moralia* 1184 b 1 ff.:
"Some goods are in the soul, such as, for instance, virtues; some are in the body, such as health and beauty;
and some are outside of us, such as wealth, office, honor,
and the like. Of these goods, those of the soul are best.
But the goods of the soul are divided into three [classes]:
philosophical knowledge, virtue, and pleasure." See further *Nicomachean Ethics* 1098 b 23 ff.; *Politics* 1323 b
1 ff. — Plato, in *Republic* 505AB, had insisted that "the
idea of the good is the highest form of knowledge,
and that all other things become useful and advantageous only through the use of this. . . . [Without this knowl-
edge] any other kind of knowledge or possession will
profit us nothing." Plato also maintains that the good is
hard to know (*Cratylus* 384AB); that it confers happiness

on its possessor (*Symposium* 204E); that it is the end
of all proper action (*Gorgias* 468B); that it is the
brightest and best of being (*Republic* 518DE); that it
is least liable to change (*Republic* 381A); and that it is
for all men an object of desire (*Euthydemus* 279A ff.;
Philebus 20D).

— 91 —

Iamblich., *Protrep.* 60,1-7; frag. 15 Walzer; frag. 15
Ross; frag. 95 Düring. — See here also Plato, *Republic*
582AB, where we are told that the pleasures of the
philosopher are the only true pleasures, because the
philosopher, and he alone, understands the meaning of
"true pleasure."

— 92 —

Iamblich., *Protrep.* 60,7-10; frag. 15 Walzer; frag. 15 Ross;
frag. 96 Düring. — See here also Plato, *Republic* 582B ff.:
"The lover of wisdom [*scil.*, the philosopher] has a great
advantage over the lover of gain. For he has a greater
experience of the pleasures [of this world] . . . All three
are honored in proportion as they attain their object;
for the rich man and the brave man and the wise man
alike have their crowd of admirers, and . . . they all
have experience of the pleasure of honor. But the delight which is to be found in the knowledge of true
being is known to the philosopher only. His experience, then, will enable him to judge better than any
other man." See also Plato, *Laws* 733E ff.; *Republic*
581D ff.

— 93 —

Iamblich., *Protrep.* 45,4-6; frag. 55 Rose; frag. 9 Walzer;

frag. 9 Ross; frag. 97 Düring. — In *Topics* 105 b 12 ff., Aristotle likewise recommends reliance on the opinions of others about certain (practical) matters. The notion of a sort of "common opinion" also appears in *Topics* 100 a 20; *Physics* 213 a 21; *Nicomachean Ethics* 1098 b 9 ff.: "We must consider . . . [the good], however, in the light not only of our conclusion and our premisses, but also in the light of what is commonly said about it. For with a true view all the data harmonize . . ."

— 94 —

Iamblich., *Protrep.* 45,6-13; frag. 55 Rose; frag. 9 Walzer; frag. 9 Ross; frag. 98 Düring. — See here also *Eudemian Ethics* 1215 b 30 ff., where Aristotle queries: "If all pleasures were removed which the intellect . . . provided men with, would a single man value life, unless he were utterly servile . . .?"

— 95 —

Iamblich., *Protrep.* 45,14-20; frag. 55 Rose; frag. 9 Walzer; frag. 9 Ross; frag. 99 Düring. — See Aristotle, *Eudemian Ethics* 1248 b 31: "Neither the imprudent nor the unjust nor the intemperate man will get any benefit from the employment of [honor, wealth, bodily excellence, good fortune, and power]. . ." See also Aristotle, *Politics* 1323 a 27 ff.: "For no one would maintain that he is happy who . . . is as feeble and false in mind as a child or a madman. These propositions are almost universally acknowledged . . ." *Nicomachean Ethics* 1147 a 14 ff.: "For outbursts of anger or passion . . . in some men even produce madness." See also Plato, *Gorgias* 512A: "A man [afflicted by a disease of the soul] had better not live, for he cannot live well."

— 96 —

Iamblich., *Protrep.* 45,21-25; frag. 55 Rose; frag. 9
Walzer; frag. 9 Ross; frag. 100 Düring. — See here Aristotle, *Eudemian Ethics* 1215 b 30 ff., quoted in comment
94, *supra*. Plato, in *Theaetetus* 173E, maintains that the
philosopher's mind, "disdaining the pettiness and nothingness of human affairs, is 'flying all about' . . . measuring
earth and heaven . . . interrogating the whole nature of
each and all . . . but not condescending to anything
which is within reach." See also Plato, *Phaedo* 83A ff.:
". . . philosophy . . . gently comforted [the soul] and
sought to release her [from her bodily confinement] . . .
persuading her to retire [from the deception of the
senses]. . . and to be gathered up and collected into herself, bidding her to trust in herself and her pure apprehension of pure existence (or, being), and to mistrust
what comes to her through other channels . . ." *Republic*
500BC: "He . . . whose mind is fixed on true being,
surely has no time to look down upon the affairs of this
world . . ." *Ibid.* at 582E, where Plato speaks of the unsurpassed delights connected with philosophic wisdom.

— 97 —

Iamblich., *Protrep.* 45,25-46,7; frag. 55 Rose; frag. 9
Walzer; frag. 9 Ross; frag. 101 Düring. — Plato, in *Theaetetus* 157E ff., holds that in dreams we have "false
perceptions." In *Republic* 571C, and *ibid.* at 574E, he
maintains that dreams are an indication of the bestial
element in human nature; and in *Laws* 910A, he states
that dreams cause superstitions. Aristotle, in *Metaphysics*
1024 b 23, insists that dreams have no connection with
truth; in *Nicomachean Ethics* 1147 a 14, he compares
a man asleep with a drunk or mad man (see also *ibid.*
at 1095 b 32); in *Magna Moralia* 1185 a 10 he denies

that a man "asleep all his life" could be called happy;
ibid. at 1201 b 17 ff., he observes that although a man
asleep has knowledge, this knowledge is not operative;
and in *Eudemian Ethics* 1219 b 18 ff., he insists that
sleep is an inactivity of the soul and that sleep reduces
us to the vegetative state. See also *Nicomachean Ethics*
1095 b 32, and *ibid.* at 1178 b 19; *Eudemian Ethics*
1216 a 2 ff.

— 98 —

Iamblich., *Protrep.* 46,8-21; frag. 55 Rose; frag. 9 Walzer; frag. 9 Ross; frag. 102 Düring. — Aristotle cites here
the basic moral tenets of ancient Greece: worship the
gods; honor thy parents; and rejoice in thy friends. See
Plato, *Laws* 716D ff. — In the *Apology* and the *Phaedo*
Plato insists that the true philosopher does not fear death,
and in the *Phaedo* he states that the wise man actually
desires death. See, for instance, *Phaedo* 61C, and *ibid.*
at 64E ff.; *et passim.* But in *Republic* 330DE, and *ibid.*
at 386A ff., as well as in *Cratylus* 403B and *Laws* 904D,
he admits that "ordinary" people are haunted by the
fear of death which is actually fear of the unknown.
The notion that man shrinks from the unknown, but naturally seeks the knowable, also appears in Aristotle,
Metaphysics 982 b 19 ff. — In *Republic* 521C, Plato
likewise maintains that philosophic learning is akin to
the soul's passing from darkness into the light of day.

— 99 —

Iamblich., *Protrep.* 46,22-47,4; frag. 55 Rose; frag. 9 Walzer; frag. 9 Ross; frag. 103 Düring. — Aristotle distinguishes here between "life as such" and "the good life,"
a distinction which also is found in Aristotle, *Politics* 1252

b 29 ff. Being tolerant, Aristotle grants that the majority of men are satisfied with "practical wisdom," with doing an "adequate job," and with "life as such." See, for instance, *Magna Moralia* 1201 a 1 ff.; *Politics* 1252 b 30 ff., and *ibid.* at 1342 a 19 ff.; *Nicomachean Ethics* 1109 b 34: "We must, as a 'second best' . . . take the least of evils." See also *ibid.* at 1109 b 19 ff.; *Magna Moralia* 1213 b 6 ff., *et passim*. See also Plato, *Laws* 687C ff. But in the main Plato insists that life is valuable only when good (*Crito* 48B); and that life is without value to the bad man (*Laws* 862E). In *Nicomachean Ethics* 1110 a 23 ff., Aristotle concedes that some people are willing to endure the greatest indignities for just a trifling end; and *ibid.* at 1179 b 4 ff., he admits that truly noble people will pursue excellence for its own sake, that is, because of the all-persuasive force or attraction of excellence.

— 100 —

Iamblich., *Protrep.* 47,5-12; frag. 59 Rose; frag. 10a Walzer; frag. 10a Ross; frag. 104 Düring. — See also Boethius, *De Consolatione Philosophiae* III. 8. — Aristotle wishes here to convey the notion that without philosophy life would not be worth living. Plato, in *Phaedo* 66B ff., informs his audience: "For the body is a source of endless trouble to us . . . and is liable . . . to impede us in the search after true being . . . and in fact . . . takes away from us the power of thinking at all . . . and by reason of all these impediments we have no time to dedicate ourselves to philosophy . . . It has been proven to us by experience that if we were to have pure knowledge of anything we must quit the body: the soul by itself must behold things in themselves. Only then shall we attain the wisdom after which we seek . . . For, if while in the company of the body, the soul cannot have pure knowledge,

one of two things follows: either knowledge is not to be at-
tained at all, or if at all, only after death." In *Eudemian
Ethics* 1215 b 18 ff., Aristotle insists that "there are many
consequences of life that make men throw away life,
such as disease, excessive pain, or storms. Hence, it is
clear that, if man were ever given the power of choice,
he would, at least as far as these reasons go, choose not
to be born at all." — Fragment 100 calls to mind Plato's
"image of the cave." Plato, *Republic* 514A, and *ibid.* at
532A ff. — See also comments to fragment 103, *infra*.

— 101 —

Iamblich., *Protrep.* 47,12-21; frag. 59 Rose; frag. 10a Walzer; frag. 10a Ross; frag. 105 Düring. — Plato (?) likewise uses the Lynceus myth in the *Seventh Epistle* 344A.
— In *Theaetetus* 173E, Plato insists that "only the outer
form [of the philosopher] is in the City [*scil.*, in this world]."
See comments to fragment 96, and Plato, *Republic* 496CD,
where Plato maintains that in this sorry world of ours
the true philosopher is "like a man who has fallen among
wild beasts" — like a man who is singly "unable to resist
the wild natures [of his fellow-man]" and, hence, "goes
his own way," being "content if only he can live his
own life and remain untouched by evil and unrighteous-
ness, and depart in peace and good-will, with bright
hopes." — Although Aristotle, on the whole, has a mod-
erately optimistic outlook concerning man, perhaps under
the influence of Plato's chronic pessimism, he occasionally
entertains pessimistic views about the "beastly" human
creature. See, for instance, *Magna Moralia* 1203 a 18 ff.:
"Again, as in the case of the vice of brutality . . . you
cannot find it in an animal, but only in a human being. . ."
Nicomachean Ethics 1150 a 7: "A bad man will do ten
thousand times as much evil as a brute beast." *Politics*

1281 a 19: "Wherein . . . do some men differ from brute beasts?" See also *Nicomachean Ethics* 1118 a 26; and *ibid.* at 1118 b 4; 1145 a 17; 1158 b 20 ff.; 1149 a 5 ff.; 1149 b 29; 1154 a 33; *Magna Moralia* 1200 b 6, and *ibid.* at 1200 b 19 ff.; *Rhetoric* 1382 b 2 ff.

— 102 —

Iamblich., *Protrep.* 47,21-48,2; frag. 60 Rose; frag. 10b Walzer; frag. 10b Ross; frag. 100 Düring. — See also Cicero, *Hortensius,* frag. 95 Müller (St. Augustine, *Contra Julianum Pelagium* IV. 15); Lactantius, *Institutiones Divinae* III. 18. — Plato, in *Republic* 330DE, admits that people near death are frightened by the punishments that may await them for their evil deeds in the "world below." About punishments in the "world below," see *ibid.* at 366A; 363D; 615A ff.; *Phaedrus* 249B; *Gorgias* 523B; *Phaedo* 108AB, and *ibid.* at 114A ff.; *Theaetetus* 177A; *Laws* 870DE, and *ibid.* at 881A; 904CD; 959B. — The notion that the body is shaped as though for punishment could be Platonic or Pythagorean (?) or Orphic (?). See Philolaus, frag. 14 (Diels-Kranz).

— 103 —

Iamblich., *Protrep.* 48,2-9; frag. 60 Rose; frag. 10b Walzer; frag. 10b Ross; frag. 107 Düring. — See also Clement of Alexandria, *Protrepticus* I. 7. 4 (p. 8 Stählin). — The notion that the union of body and soul looks very much like punishment might echo Plato, *Cratylus* 400BC: "Some say that the body is the grave of the soul which may be seen as buried in our present life . . . that the soul is suffering the punishment of sin [by being buried in the body], and that the body is a stockade or prison in which the soul is incarcerated . . . until the penalty is paid."

— See also Plato, *Gorgias* 494A ff.; *Phaedo* 62B. According to tradition, the Pythagoreans (and also Plato and Empedocles) held the view that on account of some "sin" the soul originally had been banished into the body. See Empedocles, frag. B 118, Diels-Kranz; Philolaus, frag. B 14, Diels-Kranz. Plutarch, in *Consolatio ad Apollonium* 115B-115E (where Plutarch apparently cites from Aristotle's lost dialogue *Eudemus*), insists that life as such is but a torture, and that it is better not to have been born at all.

— 104 —

Iamblich., *Protrep.* 48,9-13; frag. 61 Rose; frag. 10c Walzer; frag. 10c Ross; frag. 108 Düring. — Obviously, there is something missing between fragment 103 and fragment 104. — Plato, in *Sophist* 216BC, concludes that "divine [*scil.*, deathless] . . . is the title I should bestow on all philosophers." In *Laws* 875C, he insists that "if a man were born so divinely gifted that he could naturally apprehend the truth, he would have no need of laws to rule over him. [See also comments to fragment 37, *supra.*] For there is no law or order which is above true knowledge, nor can the pure intellect . . . be deemed the subject or slave of any man, but rather the lord and master of all. I speak of the pure intellect, true and free, and in harmony with true nature." Then, in a spirit of pessimism, Plato continues: "But then there is nowhere such a pure intellect . . ." — In *Nicomachean Ethics* 1177 a 15 ff., Aristotle calls reason "divine" or "the most divine element in us." See also *ibid.* at 1177 b 27 ff.: "If reason is divine, then . . . life according to reason is divine . . ." *Ibid.* at 1179 a 22 ff.: "He who exercises his reason . . . is most dear to the gods. For if the gods have any care for human affairs [see here Plato, *Republic* 613AB] . . . it would be reasonable that

they should delight in what was best and most akin to
them [*scil.*, reason], and that they should reward those
who love and honor this [*scil.*, the exercise of reason]
most, as caring for the things that are dear to them . . .
And that all these attributes belong most of all to philosophers is manifest." See also comments to fragment 82,
supra; Aristotle, *De Partibus Animalium* 655 a 8, and
ibid. at 686 a 28 ff.; *De Generatione Animalium* 736 b
28: "Reason is the only divine element . . . ." See also
Plato, *Republic* 013AB.

— 105 —

Iamblich., *Protrep.* 48,13-16; frag. 61 Rose; frag. 10c Walzer; frag. 10c Ross; frag. 109 Düring. — See also Epicurus,
Epistola ad Menoeceum (Diogenes Laertius X. 135);
Cicero, *De Finibus* II. 13. 40; Cicero, *Tuscul. Disput.*
1. 26. 65. — Plato, in *Phaedrus* 252D ff., points out
that "the followers of Zeus . . . have less difficulty in
finding the nature of their own God in themselves, because they have been compelled to gaze intently upon
him . . . They become possessed of him, and receive
from him their character and disposition, so far as man
may participate in God." *Theaetetus* 176AB: ". . . we
ought to fly away from the earth to heaven and become
like God, as far as this is possible; and to become like
Him is to become holy, just, and wise." *Timaeus* 90BC:
"But he who has been earnest in the love of knowledge
and of true wisdom, and has exercised his intellect more
than any other part of him, must have thoughts immortal
and divine . . . He should attain the perfect life which
the gods have held out to mankind, both for the present
and the future." See also *Republic* 500D, where Plato
maintains that the philosopher, by holding conversation
with the divine, becomes himself divine. *Ibid.* at 613AB:
"[For the just man] all things will in the end work to-

gether for his good in life as well as in death. For the
gods have a care of any whose desire is to become just
and to be like God, as far as man can attain to the
divine likeness . . . If he is like God, he will surely not
be neglected by Him." In *Metaphysics* 983 a 3 ff.,
Aristotle insists that pure philosophical speculation is the
most divine science; and in *Nicomachean Ethics* 1177 b
28 ff., he insists that "something divine is present in
man," namely, reason.

— 106 —

Iamblich., *Protrep.* 48,16-21; frag. 61 Rose; frag. 10c
Walzer; frag. 10c Ross; frag. 110 Düring. — See also Cicero,
Hortensius, frag. 97 Müller (St. Augustine, *De Trinitate*
XIV. 19. 26). — See here also comments to fragments
104 and 105, *supra*. — Plato, in *Apology* 38A, points
out that "life unexamined is not worth living." In *Crito*
48B, he insists that life is valuable only when good.
See here also Plato, *Laws* 661BD, and *ibid.* at 707D.
In *Gorgias* 512AB, he maintains that for an evil man
life is not worth living; and in *Theaetetus* 176AB, he
exhorts us to reject the ways of this world and to become like God. In brief, Plato holds that only the use
of reason, the pursuit of philosophy, makes life worth
living: true life is always the life of philosophy, and true
living is always philosophizing.